VENTURE STUDIOS DEMYSTIFIED

How venture studios turn the elusive art of
entrepreneurship into repeatable success

BY **SHILPA KANNAN & MITCHEL PETERMAN**

First paperback edition February 2022

Book design by Yeonwoo Baik
Edited by Luisa Isbell

ISBN 9798411249705 (paperback)

To inform the analysis you see throughout this book, we built a custom venture studio financial model available for download.
We recommend you explore the model and modify the various assumptions and cases to fit your own needs.

To download the free financial model template, head to our website

venturestudiobook.com

or scan the QR code below

Table of Contents

Introduction

We are fascinated by venture studios. Transforming the mythical art of entrepreneurship into a standardized process may feel impossible and even wrong to some. Entrepreneurship is hard. 90% of startups fail. Founders are lucky if they strike gold on a once-in-a-lifetime idea. You've heard this story before.

If building a successful startup is so hard, then how can one studio, one team, do it over and over again? Rightfully, it leaves many feeling skeptical. While working at venture studios ourselves, we got to peek behind the curtain and see how studios achieve this feat. However, we still left with a number of burning questions:

 What are the best ways to design and run venture studios?

 What makes a venture studio financially viable?

 How successful is the venture studio industry overall?

The more we talked with people about venture studios, the more we realized how many of them shared our questions. The industry is so new that even insiders could not answer all of them. So, we began a research project at the Stanford Graduate School of Business to answer the above questions. This book is a summary of our findings.

Our goal is to build upon the existing body of information on the venture studio landscape, not rehash accepted practices. As a result, our readers will find we have included references to additional readings throughout. If you are new to the space, we recommend starting with some context-setting white papers from GSSN, like The Rise of Startup Studios and Disrupting the Venture Landscape.

Our Methodology

We interviewed leaders at 19 different venture studios across the world, including several smaller studios still in their infancy, in order to understand challenges faced by new studio founders. We also interviewed several industry-leading studios with a larger portfolio of companies and high capitalization. We believe this sample provides a strong representation of the spectrum of the venture studio industry. We aimed to speak with a diverse group of studios across age and geographic locations to provide a wide range of perspectives and approaches to venture building. Below is a breakdown of our interviewees across these two factors:

Studio Age	%	Studio Location	%
< 5 years	32%	US	63%
5-9 years	58%	Europe	16%
> 10 years	11%	Canada	11%
		LatAm	5%
		Middle East	5%

We aggregated data on studios across a variety of categories, including

Studio structure

Recruiting

Performance

Investment strategy

Ideation process

Financing

In our analysis, we chose not to include venture studios operating within existing corporations, and instead focused on independent studios with no direct or exclusive relationship to a corporate parent. As most studios are focused on the tech industry, we intentionally focused on tech-based startup studios. Our findings may not apply to studios that launch startups predominantly in other industries, such as healthcare.

In addition to qualitative interviews, we built a sample operational and financial model to outline how some of these variables and operational decisions impact studio cash flows and return profiles. We include these findings to help provide more transparency into what makes venture studios "tick" and what operational levers to consider when working with or investing in a studio. We encourage you to play around with this model and explore how various decisions impact studio performance.

Navigating This Book

As some of our readers may not be deeply familiar with venture studios, we begin our book with context-setting. Part 1 explains what a studio is and how it differs from existing models like accelerators and incubators. Part 2 lays out some foundational industry-level knowledge, including the most common studio formation paths, strategic trends, and ideation processes.

Next, we dive into answering our first question: "What are the best ways to design and run venture studios?" In Part 3, we outline the key decisions that every studio founder has to make. We aim to highlight key operational and financial decision points, and also recognize that there are certain particulars we may not cover. We share details from our own financial model to provide context on the impact of these decisions.

We then move on to our second question: "What makes a venture studio financially viable?" In Part 4, we dive into our financial model and demonstrate how studios generate return for partners and investors. We end on our last question: "How successful is the venture studio industry overall?" We answer this with the realistic venture studio case from our model and compare it to average venture capital returns. Finally, in Part 5, we summarize all of our answers to these questions. We then synthesize our learnings and discuss the implications for different stakeholders.

As you can see, there is a substantial amount of information in the pages to come. To help readers navigate the content, each section begins with a "Section Summary" of key takeaways, followed by the details.

We tried to be as thorough as possible, however there are a number of items that warrant consideration for future research. First, studio returns data is limited and tends to only represent successful venture studios. Because of the nascency of the studio industry, we do not have consistent returns data for failed studios. As a result, we have limited ability to answer questions around which aspects of the ideation process lead to success, or the actual returns profile of the asset class. Additionally, our studio sample was skewed towards the US, which naturally limits the international applicability of our findings. Further research with more robust studio returns data would help address some of these remaining questions.

If you'd like to collaborate, or simply have additional questions after finishing this book, please send us a message at mitchelpe-terman@gmail.com and hello@shilpakannan.com. We hope this book answers your burning questions about venture studios.

Part 1:
Venture Studio Basics

Section Summary

- Studios are entities that found startups. They provide initial capital and resources for developing ideas, testing, and building products. They also assemble the founding team. In exchange for their contribution, studios are granted co-founding equity in launched companies.

- Studios are growing rapidly. The number of startup studios has grown by 625% since 2013, with 710 studios operating around the world.

- Studios are a fully-equipped team of builders and therefore much more hands-on than other sources of startup support, like accelerators and incubators. These alternatives tend to provide time-bound support through scalable programs, whereas studios design and develop their own ventures.

The Details

Venture studios are on the rise. According to Enhance Ventures, startup studios have grown in number by 625% since 2013, with 710 studios operating around the world. While the current size of the venture studio landscape is still dwarfed by the 1,965 venture capital firms in the United States alone, studio partners and investors alike are quickly realizing the benefits of moving to this model (NVCA.org, 2021).

Before we dive into what makes the studio model so attractive, we want to provide some context to readers who are new to the studio world. Idealab, one of the first venture studios, was launched in 1996. The next wave of larger, Idealab-inspired startup studios didn't come until years later, with Betaworks and Rocket Internet starting in 2007 (The Rise of Startup Studios, 2020). Many others soon followed. Although this industry has extensively developed over the past 10 years, studios as a business model are still not very well understood.

So what makes venture studios unique? They are a novel way to build startups. Studios develop venture ideas internally, conduct initial testing, build early MVPs, hire the founding team, and can even provide subsequent funding. Whereas more traditional startup founding may look like an individual entrepreneur focused on developing a single idea, venture studios instead aim to build at scale.

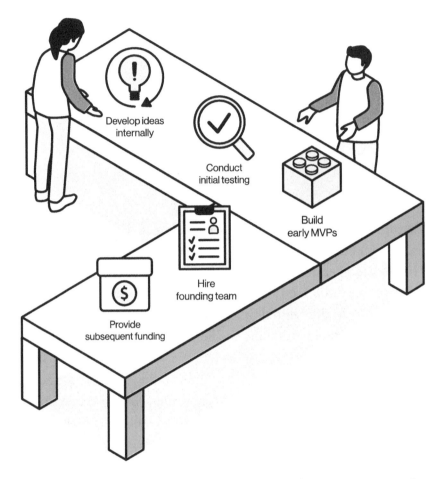

Develop ideas
internally

Conduct
initial testing

Build
early MVPs

Hire
founding team

Provide
subsequent funding

There are a few fundamental elements of any venture studio. First, studios operate as founders of their companies. Studios put in substantial time and effort into ideation, testing, and prototyping. Sometimes this is done in partnership with a chosen entrepreneur, and other times the studio conducts this early work independently.

Second, studios develop a repeatable venture-building process to enable them to launch company after company. Studios specifically design their processes to reduce the probability of failure. This includes evaluating product-market fit upfront via user research, and implementing stage gates to prevent bad ideas from advancing too far in the process. Additionally, studios tend to be founded by investors or previous founders, many of whom have experience identifying and overcoming common mistakes new founders often make. Studios leverage these learnings to increase the chances of company success.

Lastly, studios take a founding equity stake in their launched companies in exchange for their efforts. Compared to venture capital, where investors get access to companies after their creation and some level of development, studio equity is priced at nearly $0 at issuance. This provides strong financial upside to studios that hold large initial shares of venture ownership.

Beyond the attractive financial aspects, studios positively contribute to entrepreneurial ecosystems. Because studios initially "foot the bill" by funding venture ideas, entrepreneurs who join studio companies do not have to worry about bootstrapping or pulling from savings. As a result, studios open up the entrepreneurship experience to individuals who may be more financially constrained. Studios also share support and expertise with aspiring entrepreneurs who feel they do not have adequate experience to build a startup themselves. As new startups achieve success, leaders can become successful venture capitalists, serial founders, or mentors, creating a flywheel effect. By condensing the time from company formation to building ventures at scale, studios are effective ways for less established ecosystems to grow, in both the US and abroad.

With these basic characteristics in mind, let's explore how studios differ from other startup support models like incubators and accelerators.

Comparison to Other Models

Studios are unique compared to existing models, but the differences are not well understood due to the industry's nascency. Below is a graphic that highlights some of the key differences.

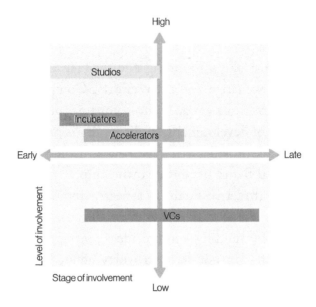

Accelerators have become well known through brand names like Y Combinator and Techstars. The accelerator model is premised on a repeatable short-term program that accepts a cohort of startups. Throughout the timeframe of the program, typically 3-6 months, founders receive mentorship and resources. In exchange for the support they receive, startups give up equity in the range of 5-10%. At the end of the program, there is often a mechanism to help the startups raise additional funding. In terms of stage, accelerators will focus on growing startups that already have a basic concept or product and spend most of their time moving from validation to customer acquisition.

This contrasts with studios, which focus on everything from ideation through customer acquisition. Company support from accelerators is typically restricted to active participation in the program, whereas studios frequently provide significant support to their companies post-launch. As a result, accelerators play a volume game. Compared to a studio, accelerators support a greater number of startups (YC's summer 2021 cohort was 377 companies) with a smaller portion of equity in each. Some studio leaders we spoke with considered moving to an accelerator model because placing more bets allows them to reduce consolidated risk. The lower support and effort required per company also means the impact and experience of personnel is more scalable.

Incubators can vary substantially, but for the most part operate in a similar fashion to accelerators. In fact, often the term incubator is used synonymously with accelerator. The main difference between incubators and studios is that incubators work with earlier stage companies. Incubators may not have structured programs and may have more flexible support timeframes. They often provide mentorship through their network and basic resources like co-working space and some operational support. Incubators typically do not generate ideas in house. Instead, they support entrepreneurs with existing ideas. As a result, incubators similarly take a smaller ownership stake, often between 5-15%. While incubators may operate at a company stage more closely aligned with venture studios, incubators are more similar to accelerators in their economics and operational models (Lesage, 2020; Prater, 2019).

Furthest away from the studio model are venture capital (VC) funds. The goal of VC is to provide funding for startups. While VCs do provide support through their network and community, it is on a more ad hoc basis than studios. VCs may provide advice on product or strategy, but unlike a studio they will not take on the role or responsibilities of a true co-founder. VCs are financiers, and while most early stage venture capitalists will hold board seats in the venture, they are not involved with day-to-day company operations.

Now that you understand the basic foundation of what a studio does and how it is unique, we will dig into the complexity of the space. Varying corporate structures, areas of specialization, and approaches to ideation and ownership can make the model diffi-cult to grasp for both investors and entrepreneurs. There are also many preconceived notions about studios and limited information on what it takes to run a successful one. The rest of this book aims to make the studio model more transparent and shed light on some of these misconceptions.

Part 2:
The Studio Approach

Now that we've covered the basics of venture studios and how they differ from other startup structures, we'll go one level deeper. In this section, we'll provide background on how studios form, recent trends in studio strategy, and the ideation process.

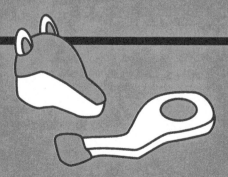

Studio Formation
Section Summary

- When studios are formed, their focus is determined by the background and skillset of the founder.

- To increase likelihood of success, we recommend studio founders build teams that draw from each focus area to maximize prior experience and diversify areas of specialization.

- Across the studios interviewed, we found three categories of studios with corresponding strengths and weaknesses.

Category	Studio Founding Description	Strengths	Weaknesses
Serial Entrepreneurship	Successful entrepreneurs looking to replicate and scale their venture creation	• Ideation • Recruiting • Startup operations	• Lack of asset management experience, leading to fundraising challenges
Investing background	Former VC investors who believe studios are a way to "de-risk" investments	• Market knowledge • Asset management experience • Fundraising	• Less expertise with early ideation, making it harder to build out an idea funnel
Product development and engineering	Dev agencies realize they can have better economics by building their own products	• Product development & testing • Technical savvy	• Limited experience with market validation • Less experience in recruiting and strategy

16

The Details

One of the first questions people ask about venture studios is simply, "where do they come from?" Who starts them and why are they well equipped to do so? We find independent studios originating from three broad areas of focus: serial entrepreneurship, investing background, and product development and engineering. We have seen successful studios emerge across all of these focus areas, and many studios have overlap across categories.

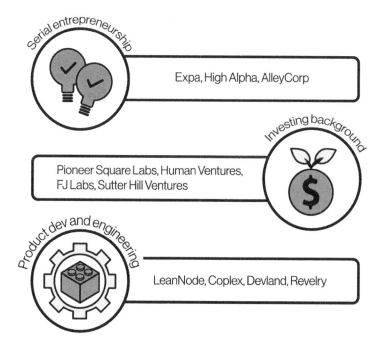

1) Serial Entrepreneurship

The most common category of studio origination stems from a focus on serial entrepreneurship. These studios are typically formed by successful entrepreneurs looking to replicate and scale their success and approach to venture creation. Expa (Garrett Camp), High Alpha (Scott Dorsey), and AlleyCorp (Kevin Ryan) all fall into this category. Studio founders with significant experience starting and operating companies are seen as proven commodities and may have an easier time raising initial funds.

On the other hand, these founder profiles may have a more difficult time raising capital for an associated VC fund due to a lack of asset management experience. Studios in this bucket may be more likely to focus on internal idea generation and prioritize heavy involvement with a smaller number of ventures. Studios with a strong former founder presence may have a comparative advantage in the ideation process, recruiting, and operational guidance.

2) Investing Background

Other studios form based on a close association with more traditional venture investment. These may start as offshoots of traditional venture capital firms, or by studio founders who either come from investing backgrounds or apply an investor-centric mindset to venture building. Pioneer Square Labs, Human Ventures, FJ Labs, and Sutter Hill Ventures all embody aspects of this category. For leaders coming from a traditional venture background, the studio model is an attractive way to "de-risk" investments. Having seen and invested in companies over their careers, VC leaders have a sense for why investments succeed or fail. VC leaders who move to found studios can leverage that knowledge to create companies more likely to be successful.

While often heavily involved in co-creation, studios in this realm may align more closely with the traditional venture playbook of placing a large number of small bets. They may also be more likely to invest in externally generated ideas or adopt accelerator-type programs. In many instances, these studios have large investment arms or significant capital available to fund external ventures or subsequent rounds of internally developed ventures. These studios may have a comparative advantage in market knowledge, pattern recognition, asset management experience, and fundraising.

3) Product Development and Engineering

Some studios began as agencies focused on product development and engineering. Given the nature of the technical work, agencies developed core competencies in helping to rapidly and efficiently build MVPs and prototypes for early-stage startups. In exchange for these services, agencies traditionally receive standard cash-based revenues. Over time, these agencies realized they could apply these specialized skills to develop prototypes and test ideas of their own. This helped advance concepts they had direct ownership in, rather than concepts solely owned by external clients. Studios like LeanNode, Coplex, Devland, and Revelry fall into this bucket. These studios tend to have a comparative advantage in development and testing, often having deep in-house technical talent or extensive networks of engineers to apply to internally generated ideas. However, studios in this category may have less experience with what comes after product build, like validation and venture scaling. When asked about product development and engineering and why it makes their studio stand out, Miles Dotson of Devland shared:

"We think innovation is a very difficult undertaking and want to make sure we are locking in on individuals and teams that demonstrate competencies and process-oriented behaviors that can break through barriers. Honestly, we believe in developing a Ph.D. equivalence in terms of the expertise level... These individuals are able to approach commercialization and market entry through rapid validations and real experiences without getting stuck on a specific angle of their initial idea."

- Miles Dotson, Managing Partner at Devland

New venture development and studio operations require a broad range of services and knowledge to successfully support startup creation. The above areas represent critical strengths each studio needs to have. We recommend studio partnerships and new studio founders build teams that draw from each focus area to maximize prior experience and diversify areas of specialization.

Strategy
Section Summary

▣ Venture capital is incentivized to grow capital under management to generate more carry dollars. Fund size and size of deals has been increasing in venture capital, resulting in round size increases over the last decade.

▣ The venture studio model is premised on generating returns by receiving cheap initial ownership, not through writing large checks. However, studio ownership gets heavily diluted in subsequent rounds.

▣ In reaction, we are seeing a convergence of the studio and VC model. Many studios are raising funds to invest in later rounds to maintain their ownership levels.

The Details

When attempting to understand the venture studio model and how it fits into the existing startup ecosystem, it's helpful to look at venture capital as a familiar reference point. Studios and VC firms are similar in function, both spurring entrepreneurship in exchange for ownership. However, their approaches are quite different.

Early stage VCs operate on the "first floor," often participating in Seed or Series A investments. From a returns perspective, while earlier stage VCs capitalize on low initial valuations, the absolute amount of money they invest at the Seed stage in each company is traditionally relatively small.

But recently, the VC industry has been undergoing a particular type of growth. Total assets under management across venture capital firms are rising at a quickening pace.

US Venture Capital AUM by Year

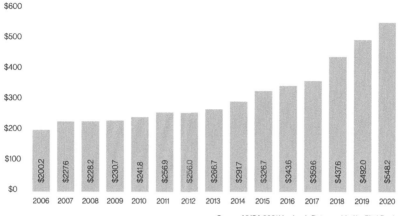

Source: NVCA 2021 Yearbook, Data provided by PitchBook

The growth in capital invested has recently far surpassed the growth in deal count. As the proportion of capital invested in deals increases, a smaller number of companies are getting more money. This means both increases in the number of mega-deals (over $100M in investment, these deals now account for 44% of all VC capital invested) and round sizes at earlier stages.

US VC Deal Flow

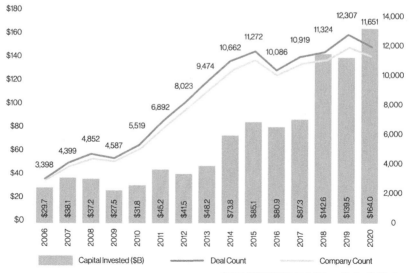

Source: NVCA 2021 Yearbook, Data provided by PitchBook

In addition, more capital is being raised through a smaller number of funds. According to the National Venture Capital Association, 2020 saw a 36% year-over-year decrease in funds closed but a 30% year-over-year increase in capital raised (NVCA Yearbook, 2021).

So what does all of this mean? As VCs have started to raise larger funds, they face the challenge of deploying their substantial capital. They address this in two ways. First, we are seeing many VC firms starting to invest in later stage companies. Later stage companies require more capital than earlier stage companies, so they present an easier opportunity for VC funds to deploy their capital. Second, we are seeing VC firms write larger checks, even at the early stages. Over the last 10 years, the median Seed size increased by 300% to $2M (PitchBook, 2021). GPs of funds have an incentive to grow their capital because more dollars at work leads to more absolute returns, which leads to more carry.

On the other hand, venture studios are based on the idea of generating return by acquiring substantial ownership early in the venture lifecycle. Studios move downstream by building or co-building ventures themselves and getting in at a company's "ground floor," when valuations remain minimal and the studio can receive cheap equity. The studio also does not need to see massive returns to be successful. Even company exits at $50M or $100M represent 50x or 100x returns! Additionally, by controlling the initial company vision, product, and leadership selection, the studio can significantly de-risk the venture and increase the likelihood that their companies receive external funding and achieve target returns. According to GSSN, 60% of startups founded out of studios reach Series A. This is a 44% improvement over non-studio-founded companies (Disrupting the Venture Landscape, 2020). This initial approach allowed studios to assume a disruptive role to traditional VCs, targeting overlooked segments of the VC market downstream, focusing on lower-cost ownership opportunities, and maintaining their unique value as they later move upstream (Christensen, 2015).

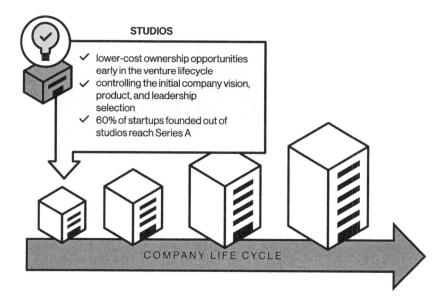

However, studios have recently seen the financial limitations of this model. Because exits take a lengthy time to materialize, all company building costs are front-loaded. The studio needs to find patient sources of capital to fund its operations for several years before seeing returns. Though a studio may start at a ~30-45% equity stake at founding, over time that stake is diluted as VCs and new employees take pieces of the pie. At exit, a studio's ownership stake could be as low as 5%. In comparison to VC funds, studios are putting extremely small amounts of capital to work and their returns are similarly limited.

In reaction to these limitations, we've recently seen a convergence in the models as studios are raising investment funds of their own. This can provide benefits in a few key ways. First, if studios charge management fees, those fees can often fund a substantial part of studio operating expenses. For example, 6 studios out of the 11 that we interviewed have funds used management fees to offset expenses. This helps extend the studio runway and reduces the need for short-term liquidity events from portfolio companies. Second, participating in subsequent post-Seed financing rounds enables studios to capitalize on their pro-rata allocation and maintain their ownership stake rather than being heavily diluted. In our interviews, we heard multiple studio leaders state they try to maintain their 20% ownership stake by continuing to invest their pro-rata over time. While this means investing at more expensive valuations, it also means the studio can see higher absolute returns at company exit. According to the National Venture Capital Association, the median VC startup exit value in 2019 was $369M in IPOs and $100M in M&As. If a VC firm maintains a 5% ownership stake at the time of exit, this would result in average returns to the fund of $18M and $5M, respectively (NVCA Yearbook, 2021). In our model, each exit would result in $22M of income to the studio. You can see how the studio model combined with a fund provides benefits to investors.

Raising funds enables studios to start to see that level of return. And for studio leaders, the compensation is unmatched. Not only do they receive carry economics in the fund, they also receive founding common equity from the studio. From our interviews, we saw that 11 out of 19 studios already have a VC fund and 4 more are planning to raise in the near future.

Interestingly, some studios are getting even closer to VC by allowing their fund to invest outside of their own studio companies. Of the studios we interviewed, ~50% currently use funds to invest outside the studio and one additional studio plans to do so. This is one way for studios that have excess funds to deploy their capital in a way that generates high returns.

We expect this convergence between VC and studios to continue as more capital flows into the asset class and more studios raise separate investment funds.

Process
Section Summary

- Studio processes leverage design thinking principles of rapid prototyping and iteration. They aim to kill unsuccessful ideas early to preserve funding for successful ideas.

  - Companies founded out of studios have a 30% higher conversion rate between Seed and Series A (72% vs 42%) (Disrupting the Venture Landscape, 2020).

- Process variation comes in the form of studios' stage gates and idea evaluation criteria.

- Process KPIs:

Funnel

 30-107 top-level ideas required to launch 1 company

Time to launch

 ~6-18 months to Seed and an additional 12 months to Series A

Companies launched

 Most studios (11 of 19) launch <4 ideas per year

The Details

Studios tend to broadly follow the same ideation and development process built on design thinking. The foundation of the design thinking process is simple: rapidly prototype, test, and fail fast. Given that studios need to fund and support ideas for several years before seeing a single exit, minimizing costs to extend funding runway is critical. Many ideas are killed in the earliest research stages, and advanced ideas are heavily scrutinized against short-term evaluation periods. It's no surprise then that studios are leveraging the design thinking process, as rapid iteration to test ideas is key in ensuring studios move nimbly without sinking too much funding into any one failing idea.

The key steps we've observed are: 1) brainstorming and early idea development, 2) customer validation (user research, testing click-through rate from social media marketing), and 3) building and testing early prototypes.

Of course, while the overall process was common across studios, we did observe some variation in the details of how they are implemented. Studios differed in the gates they set for ideas to advance or receive additional funding. These gates could include everything from securing an LOI from a customer to seeing a target click-through rate on digital marketing ads. Studios also differed in whether they had strict evaluation criteria to advance an idea, IC review, or simply increase investment by gut feel. We can see this variation through the ideation funnel, time to launch, and companies launched per year.

- Funnel: Anywhere from 30-107 top-level ideas were required to launch 1 company. A more efficient funnel means each launched idea requires less time from studio team members, and thus each idea is lower cost.

- Time to launch: Generally we saw anywhere from 6-18 months to Seed and an additional 12 months to Series A. GSSN found on average 11 months to Seed and 15 incremental months to Series A (Disrupting the Venture Landscape, 2020). Having a shorter runway to launch leads to shorter timelines for later rounds, and eventually a faster exit for the studio.

- Companies launched: We received data from 15 studios about how many companies they aim to launch per year. That data is below. The vast majority aim to launch at most 4 ideas per year, but a few studios are outliers in launching 6 or even up to 12 companies in the same timeframe. We believe this variation is attributable to 1) a differentiation in process which may enable studios to move faster than their competitors, or 2) a different bar for what constitutes a "good enough" idea to launch (studios that launch more ideas may have lower quality requirements for launch).

# ideas launched per year	Proportion of studios
At most 4	73%
4-6	13%
10-12	13%

Process variation, as well as the composition of the team, could be a main source of studio differentiation. However, studios as an asset class are young, so it is difficult to conclude whether the differentiation in process and execution directly translates to increased success or higher returns.

Part 3:
Founder Decisions

In this section, we aim to answer our first question: "What are the best ways to design and run venture studios?" We cover several key decisions that studio founders must make, both operational and financial. To help our readers navigate this wealth of information, below is a tear sheet of the decision points and main choices for each. All data points for studio breakdowns are culled from our research.

Decision Point	Choices		
Ideation process	All studios followed a similar general ideation process based on design thinking that included three steps: 1) brainstorming and early idea development, 2) customer validation, and 3) building and testing early prototypes. Usage of sprints and various decision gates in the idea selection process may differ across studios.		

Operational Decisions

Decision Point	Choices		
Industry focus	**Specialized** The most common specialization was B2B SaaS, representing 21% of interviewed studios. Specialization may allow for competitive advantage in industry knowledge but may also constrain the idea funnel, making it harder to launch companies at volume.	**Agnostic** Broader industry focus may allow for a wider idea pipeline and a larger pool of potential talent. Agnostic may be preferential if the studio team lacks industry-focused expertise.differ across studios.	
Founder sourcing	**Structured programs** Formalize programs to onboard founders.	**Limited full-time positions** Hire a small handful of founders (2-4) on an ad hoc basis.	**Assigning founders to established concepts** Hire external talent when it is time to assign a CEO to a validated idea. Studios often have their own internal business design teams for ideation and initial building.
Founder cash compensation	**Full-time employees with a set salary** Salaries are in line with the market, sometimes >$150K. No time limit, but the expectation is to launch within a year.	**Term based contractors** Paid a monthly or full-term stipend for ~6-12 months.	
Third-party agencies	**Selectively outsourcing to partner agencies** It's most common for studios to outsource engineering work and keep internal teams for ideation, recruiting, and admin.	**Fully internal teams (no third-party usage)** Some studios retain full internal teams with in-house development.	

Financial Decisions

Revenue generation	**Billing back** Charge launched companies for the services provided by studios. Usually studios only recoup a portion of costs.	**Corporate co-builds** Launch companies in partnership with established corporations. Charge a fee at ~30-50% margins and take founder equity.	**Corporate consulting** Leverage design thinking or technical expertise to offer services to corporations for a fee.
Structure	**Dual-Entity** Separate legal entities for the fund and studio-operating company. Typically, the operating company receives founder shares and the fund receives preferred equity.		**Single Fund Entity** A single legal entity where the fund and studio are not separable. This is most common with open-ended fund structure.
Fund type	**Open-ended (evergreen)** Funds without rigid liquidation expectations. Successful exits get funneled back into the fund for future investment. Some studios offer dividends on preferred shares (5-20%) to meet investor liquidation expectations.		**Close-ended** Funds intended to create a set number of companies over a certain duration. Comparable to traditional VC fund structure. Fund size varied from $10M-20M (first time funds), $50M-100M (second time funds), to $100M-200M (third time funds).
Studio financing	Most studios raise ~$10M-20M from investors for the operating company, with larger outlier studios raising $50M.		
Equity ownership	Most studios take 25-40% equity ownership (after option pool allocation). We estimate that the minimum equity stake studios can take is 10% in order to make the model work. Equity splits within a studio vary on a venture-by-venture basis depending on founder background, upfront studio work completed, compensation expectations, etc. There is significant variation in equity, ranging from 5-50% depending on these factors.		
Exit outcomes	**"True" exit (M&A, IPO)** Relevant to vast majority of studios and the timeline is highly variable (4-10 years).		**Secondary sales** Early sale of a studio's equity shares to a company or other investors. Much less common and results in smaller, faster exits. One studio achieved 5 exits in 10 years.

Part 3a:
Operational Decisions

Industry Focus
Section Summary

- ~50% of studios are vertical agnostic.

  - Given that studios need ~30-100 ideas to produce one launched company, teams can run out of opportunities if they specialize.

  - Studio focus is informed by the founder. Founders without specialized industry experience tend to be industry agnostic.

- Expect to see more studios become industry agnostic as competition increases.

- Of studios that specialized, B2B SaaS was the most common focus (4 out of 19 studios) due to business model scalability and low upfront capital requirements.

The Details

Given the substantial upfront costs in the studio funding model and the benefits of minimizing costs, we expected to see a strong bias for industry and business model specialization. Focusing on particular industries or business models would enable studios to develop specialized knowledge, foster a network from which to source entrepreneurs, understand sources of differentiation, and eventually replicate the company building process faster and more successfully over time. However, across our interviews, we saw ~50% of studios declaring a specific focus.

One of our hypotheses for this surprising conclusion is that there may be only so many promising ideas in each focus area. Given that the funnel of venture studio ideation requires ~30-100 ideas to produce one launched company, studios can rapidly run out of opportunities if they focus on too few industries. Studios are limited by the size of their staff and their own creativity. Traditional venture capital can source potential investments from entrepreneurs and visionaries from around the globe. Studios focused on in-house ideation can generally only pull from the minds of their own employees. Because of these inherent constraints to ideation and the large supply of ideas needed, we might see more studios "de-specialize" and become industry agnostic as competition increases. Additionally, studio focus is often informed by the founder. The founder's network and know-how are the foundation for the studio's ability to generate differentiated ideas, provide support, and help fundraise. If studio founders do not have specialized industry expertise, they are likely to found generalized studios.

Within studios that did specialize, the most common focus was unsurprisingly B2B SaaS. B2B SaaS represented 4 of the 19 studios we interviewed (High Alpha, eFounders, FutureSight, and Rule1 Ventures). B2B SaaS business models are known to be sustainable, typically subscriptions combined with business contracts that result in locked-in recurring revenue over time. After achieving product-market fit, scaling a B2B SaaS businesses is almost like following a playbook. Compared to D2C businesses where reaching monetization can be more difficult, or hardware businesses where substantial cash and time investment are required to build a product, B2B SaaS businesses are naturally suited for the repeatability required by the venture studio process. Quentin Nickmans, founder and managing director at eFounders, described their rationale for focusing on B2B SaaS.

> When we first came across the SaaS model in 2011, it seemed like a perfect match. Selling software to SMBs was not just about developing a product, but its success also lied in the go-to-market strategy. We were thus immediately drawn to this type of venture. Over time, there were so many opportunities in the SMB B2B SaaS space that we became very knowledgeable about what worked and how to execute it.

> - Quentin Nickmans, Founder and Managing Partner at eFounders

Working With Founders
Section Summary

- Studio leaders expressed achieving higher levels of success by bringing founders on as early as possible, even if it means less equity.

- Studios target second time founders, although they are more difficult to recruit and may command higher equity share.

- Certain studios are considering adopting accelerator-type programs, like YC, that allow them to support a greater number of new ventures for less equity (~10%).

- Studios work with external founders in one of three ways:

Approach	Description	Pros	Cons
Structured founder programs (7 of 19 studios interviewed)	Formalized program to select and onboard a specific type of entrepreneur.	• Very scalable • Lowest incremental investment per entrepreneur	• Highest upfront investment required
Limited full-time positions (7 of 19 studios interviewed)	Studios have internal ideation programs and bring on founders for certain use cases, typically 2-4 at a time.	• Attractive to high quality founders	• Founder-led ideas may have higher risk profile
Assigning founders to established concepts (5 of 19 studios interviewed)	Studios do upfront ideation and testing. Once an idea is far enough, studios recruit an external founder.	• Robust internal ideation process	• Requires most tailored effort

39

The Details

Talent and recruiting are crucial not only to a studio's operations, but also to the value they add to their co-founders. Incorporating external talent is inevitable as studios search for venture leaders. However, many studios look to external talent to help with ideation as well. Utilization of entrepreneurs in residence, or EIRs, takes many different shapes across studios. Typically, studios work with external founders in one of three ways:

 1) a structured founder program

 2) limited full-time positions

 3) assigning founders to established concepts

There is no "superior path" here. Path appropriateness depends on the studio's philosophy. The main consideration is the "ROI." What will result in the largest number of high-quality launched companies for the lowest cost. From a financial perspective, the structured founder programs require the most upfront time and investment to build out a program. Conversely, they are also the most easily scaled. In contrast, having limited or no EIRs enables studios to invest capital in founders "on-demand." However, these studios are more limited by the size and capacity of their internal team to manage ideas.

The pros and cons of each approach are summarized below.

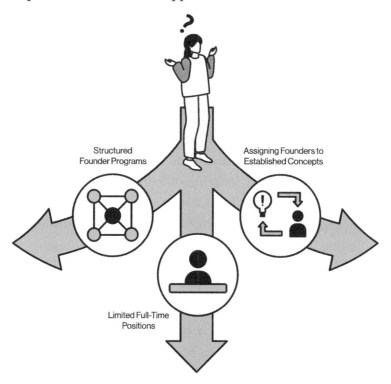

Studios with structured founder programs center their process around founder selection. The goal of the programs is to select a specific type of entrepreneur and enable their success. Because this option has the highest programmatic overhead, studios must have a repeatable process.

At the other side of the spectrum, studios that assign founders to established concepts tend to have a robust internal ideation process. Studios may choose this path for financial reasons. Because this path often requires the studio to make a greater investment in an idea and complete more work independently, they can justify a higher equity stake.

The middle path, utilizing founders in limited full-time positions, strikes a balance. Studios that operate here have internal ideation programs and bring on founders only for certain use cases. Although, because these studios are not built specifically for managing external founders, founder-led ideas may have a higher risk profile.

Structured Founder Programs

Studios who primarily rely on external founders for early ideation and validation typically feature some sort of formalized program to select and onboard early founding talent. 37% (7 of 19) of studios that we interviewed had a consistent and structured approach to incorporating external talent into the studio. One of the key differentiators for founder programs is their recruitment source. Many of these roles and programs have publicly available descriptions and applications, and the majority of participants come from inbound application submissions. Very rarely do these programs evaluate applicants with a heavy emphasis on their initial ideas. In fact, some programs don't even accept externally developed ideas. They instead focus on the candidate's experience and likelihood of success as an entrepreneur.

Founder programs are often bifurcated based on the time commitment and number of participants supported. Next Big Thing's EIR program and Human Ventures' *Humans in the Wild* incubation programs are examples of shorter, lower commitment programs that screen a larger number of potential founders or ideas to invest in. These programs provide their respective studios with a mechanism to screen initial venture concepts and trial entrepreneurs over a shortened duration (~3 months). Selected participants will often be provided strategic support and minimal funding to develop their concept. The studio then has the ability to choose whether or not to provide additional funding and "co-found" the company with the entrepreneur at the end of the program. Marc Zapp from Next Big Thing shares the benefits of a short term EIR program:

> Our main driver behind the short-duration EIR program is to identify the most promising ideas in the shortest possible time with a minimal capital contribution. The program enables just that and it gives founders a unique opportunity to challenge their professional skills and knowledge in today's dynamic business landscape.

- Marc Zapp, Senior Brand Manager at Next Big Thing

As Marc described above, these programs provide an extremely low-cost way to test early founders and concepts, while essentially outsourcing ideation efforts to a batch of potential founders. From the founder perspective, entrepreneurs early in their idea development can get support without giving up significant equity, which highlights the appeal of programs like Humans in the Wild. Human Ventures' Venture Partner Evan Cohen describes this below.

> We have always been eager to work with entrepreneurs at the very 'top of the funnel' of the build process, sometimes even before a company idea is finalized or a line of code is written. By removing the gating threshold of asking founders in our Humans in the Wild program for equity, we lower the friction to super early stage entrepreneurs joining our programs.

- Evan Cohen, Venture Partner at Human Ventures

At the same time, these programs can potentially distract from internal ideation efforts and there can be heavy administrative and personnel costs without any initial equity in return. To bypass these possible downsides, other studios build programs core to their ideation process. These programs focus on a smaller number of participants with longer contract commitments for EIRs. Studios frequently differ in how these programs utilize selected candidates. Some studios do not expect EIRs to be responsible for ideation, instead assigning them to lead an existing idea that has been internally generated. EIRs may test and validate several existing ideas before finding a viable concept they fit with. Other studios believe that the EIR needs to be involved with ideation from day zero. In these cases, the studio will enable the EIR to drive research in their areas of interest, develop and flesh out the idea and, should studio leadership approve, advance to later stages of the process.

While this amount of responsibility may seem overwhelming for some EIRs, in many instances studios do not expect them to ramp to the role of full founder immediately. Rather, they have apprenticeship-like programs where select EIR participants support existing studio ventures before working in a founder capacity themselves. FJ Labs' apprenticeship program embodies this concentrated program approach. When asked why they have founders run through an apprenticeship program rather than assigning founders to existing ideas, FJ Labs' Founding Partner Jose Marin shared:

> We believe that it's important for founders to be emotionally connected to the idea they build. If we hire and assign, then we are imposing the idea rather than evaluating a large number of them in a structured and systematic way based on the founder preference. Also, it is a perfect opportunity to have the EIRs work with us in the day to day and get to know each other better as part of a longer term relationship.
>
> - Jose Marin, Founding Partner at FJ Labs

From a financial perspective, we believe studios that choose this path may spend substantial upfront time and money iterating on the model, investing in entrepreneurs that do not pan out, and/ or initially seeing a worse "output" from the funnel. However, over time, this can become a very repeatable model with low incremental investment required in each entrepreneur.

Because of this significant investment of time and money, a number of studios are also exploring lighter touch founder programs. These programs allow them to support a greater number of new ventures without dramatically expanding studio operations. One studio that we spoke with, which usually takes 35% equity, was considering creating a 10% equity program. This studio envisioned the lower equity program as a way to provide support to a larger number of ventures, rather than being a fully involved co-founder. The advantage of this model is scalability. Large studios that have a flourishing program at some point will hit limits on how many EIRs they can support. A 10% program vastly expands the pool of ideas a studio can support with limited downside. As existing EIR programs scale, we imagine this will become a larger trend. Although, differentiation may be challenging as this model is highly similar to established startup accelerators like Techstars and Y Combinator.

Limited Full-Time Positions

A number of studios do not have established EIR programs or rolling application cycles. These studios often will hire a small handful of high-potential founders, usually 2-4 at a given time to generate ideas or work through high-potential concepts. Unlike structured founder programs, candidates for these positions are often recruited through a studio's personal network. Studios may even create databases to track high-potential founder candidates as well. These roles may not be publicly advertised, and candidates may be hired on an ad hoc basis as new individuals and ideas are introduced to the studio.

Assigning Founders to Established Concepts

Finally, there are a handful of studios that do not generally use paid EIR positions or structured founder programs. These studios place a heavy emphasis on internal idea generation and may even have robust business design teams to generate, research, and validate new concepts. 5 of the 19 studios interviewed fit these criteria, including Horizon Two Labs and High Alpha. Typically these studios will bring on external talent when it is time to assign a potential CEO to a validated idea. This newly assigned founder will then lead the venture as it works through further customer validation, early product development, and initial fundraising. While searching for company-specific leadership may allow a studio to find a CEO with a more need-based fit, there is a chance that the new leader is less personally motivated or invested. This could be because they were not present during the initial concept development.

One common trend noted by studio founders was a shift towards early team formation for new ventures. Even studios without separate full-time EIR positions expressed seeing more success when they brought a potential founding team into an idea earlier. As described by one studio founder, "The later you bring the leader to the business, the harder it is for them to put a stamp on the business." Another studio indicated how, in their first fund, the ventures without a founder/CEO in charge early tended to struggle. While bringing a founder on sooner may result in the studio giving them a higher portion of founding equity, we still observed comparable ownership levels for studios whether they brought founders on board early or assigned them later to more developed concepts. Time of founder entrance may have an impact on equity split within studios, but it appears other factors like studio's past success, reputation, and amount of initial investment play a larger role in differences in ownership share across studios.

Compensation is one of the biggest challenges expressed by studio founders, with a high impact on their ability to attract top-tier founders to EIR roles or existing ventures. Equity compensation is discussed under "Equity Ownership" in Part 3, but first we will discuss cash compensation below.

Cash Compensation

EIRs are either employed as full-time employees or term-based contractors. EIRs hired as full-time employees are often paid a set salary from the studio, typically coming from the operating budget or management fees from the studio's fund. While these employees don't typically have a set end date, the common expectation is that they will arrive at an investable venture idea within a year. If a studio determines an EIR to be high quality, they may retain them as an employee for longer. This allows them to attempt second or third ventures. Salaries are relative to the local job market but are often quite competitive, venturing north of $150,000 in major markets. This cash compensation is obviously highly appealing to potential founders as it significantly de-risks the pursuit of entrepreneurship, and is usually an accounted for expense in the studio's operating budget.

Other EIR programs have potential founders join as term-based contractors. These EIRs will either be paid a monthly or full-term stipend to work toward developing a venture. These contracts typically last for 6-12 months. Often the expectation is that an EIR may have the opportunity to try a small handful of ideas during this time, either arriving at a concept the studio will fund or being let go. There may be milestones built into the contract as well, in order to unlock increased funding or extensions. These contracts may be less risky to studios and allow them to test out more entrepreneurs, but are often less appealing to top-tier founders.

Early founders retained to work on studio ventures may continue to be paid by the studio, but more commonly take cash compensation from studio funds invested in their venture. Some studios limit the amount a founder can take as compensation, while others choose not to regulate venture spending once it has been invested. Studios have to weigh on whether they prefer to increase invested capital in their ventures to pay founder salary or continue to treat it as an expense from their operating budget.

Founder Profile

Studios bank on the hypothesis that founders, even formerly successful founders, will be willing to choose them over traditional VC investment because they provide founders with the option to work on an already "de-risked" idea with administrative support. Some studios target first-time founders with operational or industry experience, a group that is generally easy to attract given the support studios provide. In particular, studio EIR programs (such as FJ Labs or Atomic) can appeal to entrepreneurial-minded individuals who do not have a specific passion project or focus area.

However, based on our research, we found that most studios target second-time founders with proven experience. Because second-time founders generally have an existing network in the entrepreneurial and VC community, they can be more difficult to recruit. The value proposition that studios sell to these founders is that they can alleviate all administrative headaches of starting a company, enabling the founder to solely focus on building product. However, this sales pitch is heavily dependent on studio reputation and past success, the strength of studio partners' personal connections, competitive salary, and favorable equity splits to the founder. There is a narrow group of entrepreneurs that this sales pitch appeals to and they can be difficult to find. Full-time EIRs are often expected to generate an investable business concept within 6-12 months, potentially cycling through numerous ideas during that time.

Here are some terms and phrases studio founders used to describe what they look for in an EIR or founder:

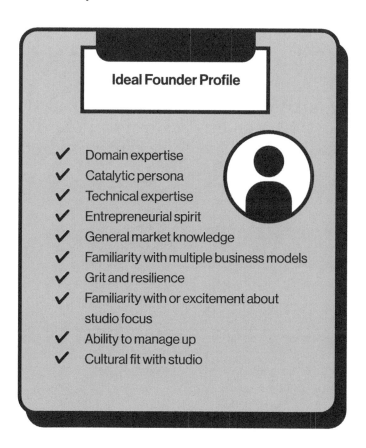

Ideal Founder Profile

✔ Domain expertise
✔ Catalytic persona
✔ Technical expertise
✔ Entrepreneurial spirit
✔ General market knowledge
✔ Familiarity with multiple business models
✔ Grit and resilience
✔ Familiarity with or excitement about studio focus
✔ Ability to manage up
✔ Cultural fit with studio

Third-Party Agencies
Section Summary

While studios initially kept all engineering, product, and design work in-house, we've started to see many studios outsource development work to third-party agencies because they are cheaper and easier to manage.

The Details

A trend we observed among some studios is the utilization of external service agencies rather than staffing and maintaining large in-house design and engineering teams. Original studio designs often incorporated full engineering, product, and design teams to build early MVPs and prototypes of venture concepts. However, several studios indicated significant challenges managing these teams that didn't justify their perceived benefits. Personnel costs to maintain these teams can be too large to be supported by management fees, or they may place significant strain on operating budgets. In addition, transitioning technical talent between studio and ventures can be difficult. This can result in studio engineers consistently leaving to join newly established ventures and leaving ventures they worked on with a significant technical gap.

For early-stage concepts, many studios decided that outsourcing development work to third-party agencies is a cheaper alternative than maintaining staff. As studios grow and develop expertise in recruitment and talent acquisition, they have also realized that it is more cost efficient and helpful to recruit engineering talent to join their venture full time, rather than providing in-house services. Studios often maintain a network of partner service agencies, many of which offer studios discounted rates. Studios either use their operating budget to pay for these services to be completed for early ventures, or they pay with a venture's allocated invested capital. Many studios are also opting to bill ventures back for these services once they have incorporated. The implications of this are further discussed in Part 3.

While some studios retain large engineering and product teams, we spoke with three studios who initially had large engineering teams and have since chosen to stop, moving to leaner teams focused primarily on ideation, recruiting, and admin (legal, HR, finance). This appears to be where a number of studios have determined their unique value proposition lies.

Part 3b:
Financial Decisions

In this section, we highlight key financial decision points that each studio faces. We will cover the choices studios have when making these decisions and trends we observed across our dataset. In the next section, we discuss the quantitative impact of these choices to help leaders concretely understand the trade-offs they face. We recommend readers spend time understanding this section before heading to the model.

Revenue Generation
Section Summary

▫ Studios face high upfront expenses and long timelines to liquidity, making cash flow an issue. Revenue generation can bridge this cash flow gap and extend studio runway.

▫ The three most common ways to generate revenue:

  ◻ Billing back launched companies can help studios cover a portion of their investment, but the exact amount of bill back varies substantially by studio.

  ◻ Corporate co-builds provide a mix of fees and equity (~30-35%) to the studio. The dependence on a corporation for idea development, and often funding and exit, make these ideas riskier.

  ◻ Corporate consulting provides substantial margins (~40%) but requires a team to be split across consulting engagements and venture building. Only 1 out of 19 studios we spoke with did this.

▫ Billing back is the preferable strategy, as it does not distract from core studio operations.

The Details

As described above, the expenses for company building (ideation, validation, etc.) are paid upfront and the salaries for personnel are constantly due. However, exits often take years to materialize, resulting in a funding gap. Generating revenue through consulting, corporate co-building, or billing back are ways to help bridge this gap.

While you might expect studios that have fundraised to have solved this cash flow issue, we were surprised to see how widespread the challenge of maintaining funding was. Even studios that have raised from LPs are laser-focused on revenue generation. One studio leader we spoke with, who is in their 6th year of operation and has raised nearly $30M to fund the studio, mentioned that they are still "trying to stretch out runway by lowering burn." Another studio that raised funds in an evergreen structure is working with corporates to generate revenue. And, for studios that were outside of major entrepreneurial hubs, the challenge was even more acute because fundraising from-risk averse investors was much more difficult. Creating a sustainable source of revenue is a way to extend the studio's life and generate more companies for the same amount of investor funds, which is something that impacts all studios.

We saw three main paths for studios to generate revenue:

Billing back   Corporate co-builds   Corporate consulting

Billing Back Startups

One option studios can pursue is to charge their launched companies for services provided. Based on our interviews, the goal of billing back is not to turn a profit but rather to reimburse the studio for costs incurred. As a result, we mostly saw studios bill back at cost or discount.

We found that 3 distinct stages separating how studios bill back:

- Pre-incorporation: When ideas are created but live under the studio brand because they are too early.

- Post-incorporation but pre spin-out: The idea is fleshed out enough that the studio decides to incorporate it as a company. As a result, the studio can start allocating expenses directly to the company. However, at this point the company still operates within the studio. The studio often tends to bring on a founding team.

- Post spin-out: At this point, the company becomes separate from the studio and operates as a fully independent company without direct studio management. As mentioned above, we saw companies spin out anywhere from 6-18 months from origination.

Of course, a key factor informing these milestones is when

incorporation and spin-out occurs. The timing of incorporation can vary substantially depending on studio preference, and we saw many instances of incorporation after validation or MVP. We primarily saw spin-out between the Seed and Series A rounds.

There is a range of approaches studios take with regards to billing back their portfolio companies, and they are detailed below.

 No bill back: On one end of the spectrum, some studios choose not to bill back for services at all. They consider their support an investment and a cost for their co-founding equity stake.

 Post spin-out bill back: Multiple studios we observed charge only for services post-spin-out, such as helping companies recruit new talent at cost. Studios justify that the early expenses were made in exchange for the founder shares, and that the company should reimburse the studio for any support provided after spin-out. This is a common approach because it is easy to justify to entrepreneurs that once the company becomes separate it needs to reimburse the studio at cost.

 Post incorporation bill back: Another common approach observed was billing post-incorporation. Studios that do this tend to charge back only a portion of services, for example engineering cost to develop an MVP. While incorporation can be an earlier point to start billing back, many studios believe these services would have to be paid for by the company regardless of whether the studio or a third party provides them. Additionally, some studios only charge back for a portion of services, so the cost to studio-founded companies is lower than what an external agency would charge. Compared with the prior choices, studios that bill back post-incorporation see higher revenue, thus making this a compelling option.

 Full bill back: The most aggressive approach we observed was billing back for all services. We only observed one studio taking this path because charging for all costs can call into question the validity of taking a substantial founding equity stake. This studio justified their position by arguing they were the primary founder and that they deserved 100% of the business, but also decided to give away some equity for the benefit of the entrepreneur. Thus, the studio should be compensated for their upfront investment. While this path worked for this one studio, we found this to be a hard sell. Studios in well-capitalized areas like the Bay Area will run into challenges with an aggressive bill back model due to the alternative capital and entrepreneurial support available.

Of these four choices, the bill back path that studios opt for tends to be a question of the studio leadership's philosophy and the studio's cash flow needs. For new studios, billing back post-incorporation can be a good starting point because it mitigates cash flow challenges while also being relatively easy to explain to entrepreneurs.

One final open question on our minds was about the interaction between billing back and equity stakes. We posited that studios that billed back aggressively, specifically pre-spin-out, would have to give up some equity as a result. However, we did not see any correlation between billing back pre-spin-out and the size of the equity stake taken by the studio. We hypothesize that paying for studio services is not a high priority consideration for founders, as a few hundred thousand for services will not make or break a company. Additionally, founders enter into partnerships with studios because they realize the value proposition of a studio is in conducting the upfront work. As a result, we imagine that some founders expect to pay for services provided.

Corporate Co-Builds

In this method, studios attempt to launch companies in collaboration with large corporations. For each stage of the funnel (ideation, validation, etc.), the studio charges the corporation at some margin above cost. We found that studios aimed to charge substantial margins, frequently in the range of 30-50%. If the idea makes it through the funnel, the company is jointly launched with the corporate partner. The studio will take an equity ownership stake, similar to internally generated ideas (~30-35% based on our interviews). Corporate co-builds may attract potential founders with big company experience who are more likely to understand and value the resources of larger organizations. 6 of the 19 studios interviewed had worked with corporations to co-build companies, including High Alpha, Prehype, and Pioneer Square Labs.

Corporate co-builds have several benefits. First, corporate partners usually have deep domain expertise that studios struggle to build. Second, from a funding perspective, corporate co-builds can have a more certain funding path since corporations are usually willing to invest in subsequent funding rounds. Lastly, if the company does well, the corporate partner could acquire the company relatively quickly, resulting in substantial cash flow and a fast, successful exit.

However, there are real downsides to corporate co-builds. While studios are generally given autonomy over the process, corporations still have a say, and this introduces unpredictability. Some studios experienced corporate partners unwilling to take the plunge and incorporate co-built companies, forcing the studio to remain squarely in the "consulting" phase. Additionally, there is an assumption that corporate partners are motivated to launch co-builds to drive internal innovation and growth for strategic value. Unfortunately, strategic value is largely irrelevant to a studio. The only way "strategic value" can be quantified is if the corporation acquires the co-builds. An example of this occurring successfully is Pioneer Square Labs (PSL). PSL launched a joint studio with Fortive corporation in 2020. Since then, the studio has launched 3 companies. The first spin-out, Teamsense, was acquired by Fortive within 18 months of company launch. This was a fast exit, proving one of the benefits we named above. While this can happen, both the studio landscape and this revenue stream are new enough that it is unclear if corporate acquisitions would be the norm. Greg Gottesman from Pioneer Square Labs shared how the perception of "strategic value" can pose a challenge for corporate co-builds:

> The biggest challenge in developing ventures with corporate partners is the same one we have building studio companies in the non-corporate context: finding exceptional talent to lead the spin-outs. In the corporate studio context, recruiting these top-notch co-founders can be trickier because their perception might be that the corporate partner will influence the spin-out in a way that could limit the upside. Our job, together with the corporate partner, is to dispel that perception and demonstrate that the corporate relationship is going to bring unique value that increases the likelihood of the spin-out's success.
>
> - Greg Gottesman,
> managing director and Co-Founder of Pioneer Square Labs

Lastly, and perhaps most importantly, a majority of venture studios use the same team members to run corporate engagements and internally driven efforts. As a result, working on corporate co-builds represents a direct trade off to launching internal companies.

Pros	Cons
• Domain expertise from the corporate partners' side	• Unpredictability from working with a corporate partner
• A more certain funding path	• Questionable strategic value
• Possibility of relatively quick acquisition by the corporate partner	• Team time that can distract from core ideation effort

Corporate Consulting

The last method of revenue generation that we observed is for studios to act as consultants. Studios have expertise in design thinking and can often support corporations in innovation and growth. Additionally, studios that started as development agencies can offer their technical talent to build products for companies. With this method, studios are trying to charge for services at a margin rather than trying to launch companies.

This path is most relevant for studios with technical expertise. In these cases, studio leaders have technical backgrounds but perhaps not the entrepreneurial experience to earn investor confidence. These studios may use consulting or agency revenue to raise cash early, before they establish a strong reputation as a venture studio. Even so, this path of revenue generation is not a common choice and only one studio we spoke with went this route. And for good reason! Though this revenue stream can be lucrative (the studio referenced makes 40% profit margins on their services), the downside is it runs counter to the company-building mission of the venture studio. These contracts can be difficult to source, difficult to execute, and extremely time-consuming, reducing how many companies the studio can realistically launch.

Managing Process Costs

The previous sections assume that the studio decides to offset costs by generating revenue. However, another path studios can take is to directly reduce the cost of their process. There are a few ways we observed studios doing this. First, studios can move to outsource some of the process to external agencies, particularly MVP or early product builds. This may actually be cheaper than maintaining full development teams (see the section "Third-Party Agencies"). Second, studios can add more go or no-go decisions earlier in the ideation process so that ideas are killed before incurring full validation and MVP costs. Go or no-go milestones differed by studio, however we did hear that some studios limit spending on ideas to $50K-100K before the first "go ahead."

Lastly, studios can replicate successful business models launched in other geographies so that less validation and MVP work is required. This is mostly relevant for studios in smaller or newer entrepreneurial ecosystems. Studios like Rocket Internet and Drukka (in its early days) built studios that implement this approach (Szigeti, 2019). The financial impact of a lower-cost process is fairly straightforward, so we have not included model comparisons here. We leave it to the reader to play around with cost assumptions.

Raising a Fund

As discussed above, many studios are moving towards having a fund so that they can deploy more dollars in spun-out companies. When studio leaders consider raising a fund, one of the first questions they must consider is how having this new entity will impact company structure. Though this may sound like a legal question, structural decisions also have wide-reaching implications on operations. Questions around employee incentivization, funding for operational growth, ease of fundraising, and returns are all dependent on the type of structure studios choose. Thus, we will start with an overview of studio structure choices before diving into fund type and studio financing.

Studio Structure
Section Summary

🔲 A review of FutureSight's outline of five different choices for studio structures.

🔲 Many studios that originated as single studio entities are migrating to dual-entity models by raising VC funds. A minority of studios utilize a single fund entity model.

	Dual-Entity Model	Single Fund Entity Model
Definition	Separate legal entities for the fund and studio operating company	Only one legal entity
Equity ownership	• The operating company receives founder shares (common equity) • Investment fund holds preferred equity from Seed and post-Seed	Returns from common and pre-ferred shares are shared across the single entity
Fund size considerations	Can grow a fund to target larger checks or follow-ons without affecting studio budget	With 2% management fees and a $2M-4M budget, fund size would need to be $100M-200M
LP challenges	Raising funds for the operating company can be challenging because it's a unique profile vs traditional VC	Raising a large enough fund size to cover operations is challenging for first-time leaders

The Details

In addition to studios' various approaches to investing, there are also different approaches to the way they are structured. We recommend reviewing FutureSight's outline of different choices for studio structures and the relative advantages and disadvantages of each to familiarize yourself with the various frameworks. Studio structure has important implications on the type and source of funding available to a studio, how they operate, and incentive alignment between participants. It can also be highly relevant for studio employees' and partners' understanding of the compensation types available to them. Deciding on structure is often one of the first decisions a new studio founder makes, and one that has lasting impact.

As we previously mentioned, we observed a migration to dual-entity models as many studios start raising VC funds, particularly for studios that originated as single studio entities. We saw a minority of studios in a single fund entity model. While this is straightforward and simplistic to implement, the limitation of funding from a single source makes this structure more broadly challenging compared to the dual-entity model.

There are a number of potential studio structures, but the majority we observed were either dual entities or single fund entities. For this reason, we chose to focus specifically on these two structures in this book. Below we will dive deep into various aspects of the dual-entity model, given that most studios opted for that structure. However, at the end of the section we have included a summary of the considerations for a single fund entity model for interested readers.

Dual-Entity Model

The core of the dual-entity model is establishing separate legal entities for the fund and studio operating company. The operating company tends to receive founder shares (common equity) in the launched companies, whereas the investment fund tends to hold preferred equity from Seed and post-Seed investments. As a result, the investment profile of the operating company and investment fund are quite different. The operating company provides direct economic ownership in portfolio companies whereas the fund is more similar to traditional VC economics (2% management fee, 20% carry).

Studio Leadership

In most dual-entity models, partners remain the same across both the operating company and the investment fund. While some funds may have a separate investment committee that includes other studio personnel, the partner group is usually common across the operating company and fund. The investment committee of the fund establish criteria for companies to receive investment, similar to how studios do so for companies to pass through process gates.

A particularly appealing trend for studio partners and leadership is the ability to participate in the economic upside of both the operating company and the fund. In many instances, partners receive a portion of the carry generated by the fund while also being allocated direct equity ownership in newly created portfolio companies. In this way, partners are able to "double dip," making the model particularly lucrative (arguably more so than traditional VC fund management, if the studio is successful). In some cases, studios are using special purpose vehicles to allow individual studio partners to hold equity directly in portfolio companies as well. Below the studio leadership, it was highly variable whether employees received carry in the fund or equity directly into portfolio companies. We observed instances where employees received direct economics in launched companies, and others where employees were only compensated in cash. Compensation to studio team members is likely driven by the surrounding market environment rather than any particular industry best practice.

Development Costs

Dual-entity studios often pay for early ideation and company creation efforts from the balance sheet of their operating company. The operating company cash is grown through a mix of sources: funds raised, revenue the studio earns through external services or corporate builds, and/or a portion of the management fees (2%) of the studio's investment fund.

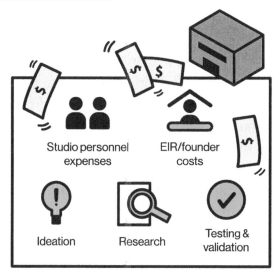

The operating company's budget can help cover studio personnel expenses, EIR/founder costs, ideation and research, and early consumer testing and validation. If there are separate close-ended funds within the studio, this broader operating budget may cover expenses across all sub-fund activities as well. The studio receives common founder shares in return for funding these early operations for portfolio companies, which is colloquially referred to as "pre-Seed" funding. This funding takes the company through Seed, at which point we see the first real investment from the studio fund in the form of a convertible note into preferred equity. We mentioned this separation above, how generally the operating company holds the common and the investment fund holds the preferred, with occasional exceptions.

Startup Fundraising

With respect to funding, one important area of divergence is when external capital is brought in to fund portfolio companies. The vast majority of studios we spoke with only saw their companies bring in external investors to lead funding at the Series A. This ensures that the studio has an opportunity to build up cheap equity before getting diluted. However, we did see a small number of studios start to bring in external VCs to lead the Seed. Immature studios or studio leaders that are worried about the strength of their reputation may decide it is beneficial to bring in external capital earlier to help signal validation to the market. Some studios solely focused on idea generation may also only choose to support ventures until they incorporate and become independent. While the trade-off is a lower initial equity stake, external funding could result in external signaling and validation that leads to company success down the round.

In some instances, we saw studios providing early investment in their ventures from funds in the form of a convertible note. This is provided in exchange for a portion of the operating company's founding equity share. This was primarily driven by shared economics between the fund and operating company, and an effort to leave enough ownership available for founders and subsequent investors.

The dual-entity model becomes particularly beneficial for studio founders deciding between raising a fund or increasing the amount of money on their operating company balance sheet. If studio founders are looking to participate in their ventures' fundraising rounds, having a structured fund allows partners to receive carry and management fees for their investment. By simply investing off the balance sheet, studio partners would essentially be providing asset management services without any of the secondary compensation.

Fund Ownership in Studio

One of the decision points for dual-entity structures is whether the investment fund will invest and own equity in the studio operating company. A benefit of the fund owning part of the operating company is that fund LPs are aligned and invested in the success of the studio. Funds that do not own equity in the studio may be more solely focused on the fund's investments, not the entire studio portfolio or venture creation capacity. For LPs, a key benefit is their exposure to not only preferred equity, but also common equity through the studio holding company. Additionally, from the perspective of the management team, having the fund Seed part of the studio lightens the load for how much the studio operating company needs to raise.

However, there are downsides. Placing fund investment into studio operating company ownership makes the fund profile less similar to traditional VC, which can make fundraising more challenging. Allocating some of the initial fund capital to the studio also means fewer funds are available to invest in portfolio companies, resulting in lower ownership percentages and likely smaller exits. We encountered both situations in our research. We are curious to see whether the industry moves toward fund ownership in studio operating entities or not.

Studio Carry

In some instances where partners are shared across the fund and the operating company, studio leadership will also choose to allocate a portion of the carry from the fund to the operating company. This is to help grow venture development capacity and allow operating company staff to share in future venture success. We observed this in only a few cases, as transferring carry to the operating company can be complicated and GPs may not want to reinvest their economics.

Single Fund Entity Model

We saw a minority of studios choose to remain as single fund entities. The idea behind a single fund model is that there is only one legal entity. The fund and the studio are not separable. While the fund technically could be closed or open-ended, in our research we typically saw single fund models use an open-ended structure in the form of evergreen funds.

Studio Leadership

In a single entity model, a partnership or ownership structure is established for the entity and typically oversees all studio operations, including both venture building and investing.

Development Costs

A benefit of the single entity model is that it is straightforward to understand and implement. The downside is that there is only one entity from which to fund studio operations and studio investments into the portfolio. Management fees (2%) are typically used to cover expenses incurred before a new venture incorporates (personnel and ideation), while post-incorporation costs typically come from the fund's investable capital. As a result, single fund studios require a large fund size to support high upfront incubation and venture development costs. This can make starting as a single fund entity quite difficult, especially for first-time studio founders. However, for studios able to raise enough initial capital to fund idea development, the simplicity of single fund structures can be highly appealing.

One way to help mitigate this challenge is by structuring as an open-ended fund. This can be particularly valuable for studio leaders with entrepreneurial experience but a less proven track record of investing. Since open-ended funds heavily support venture building and operating activities, LPs are actually investing in the studio leadership's operating capabilities and thus may be more flexible with respect to investing experience. In fact, one of the studios we spoke with stated that they utilized the open-ended single fund structure because "[we] received feedback that [we] had a good track record of building, but not so much as an asset manager...we did a holding company so [LPs] would invest in [us] as a builder and less as an asset manager."

Though single fund entities have the benefit of simplicity, their limitation is that all funding needs to come from the investment fund, including capital to fund the studio. LPs from the investment fund would likely only allow management fees to cover studio operations. Given annual operating expenses are anywhere from \$2M-4M for a studio, fund sizes would have to be \$100M-200M in a single fund entity (accounting for 2% management fees). Wenyi Cai of Polymath Ventures, a studio structured as an evergreen company, described the limitations of a single fund model:

> We chose the evergreen company structure to give us flexibility in the allocation of capital towards building new companies or investing and supporting existing ventures. The cost of building just doesn't fit well within a 2% fee structure. In addition, the valuation of a company is more consistent with how we create value, instead of the 20% carry structure for deployment of capital.
>
> - Wenyi Cai, Founder and CEO of Polymath Ventures

For studios that can raise such a large fund at inception and have LP agreements in place to ensure that the fund/studio retains the majority of returns, a single fund structure is suitable. However, as described below, most studios will not see fund sizes of \$100M-200M until at least the third or fourth fund. Thus, in the vast majority of cases, if a studio has a fund it should use a dual-entity structure. While the dual-entity structure introduces more complexity, it enables leaders to raise funds separately for the operating entity.

Startup Fundraising

In this model, early capital provided to new startups and subsequent investment in following rounds simply comes from the fund. In some instances, later stage growth investments in existing ventures may come from a studios separate and larger growth fund.

Fund Ownership in Studio

In a single entity structure, all equity is held by the same entity since the fund and operating company are the same. Returns to the fund can be used to further fund studio operations and Seed additional new ventures.

Studio Carry

Similar to a dual-entity model, studio partners may choose to either reinvest carry back into studio operations or distribute among studio personnel.

Fund Type
Section Summary

Investment funds can be structured as either open-ended (evergreen) or closed-ended funds. Most studios interviewed selected a closed-ended fund.

Evergreen funds provide studio leaders the most flexibility, but it is harder to attract LPs because it is not a most commonly-accepted VC investing structure.

In an evergreen fund, all portfolio exits go back into the fund and grow investing capital.

Studios may offer investors guaranteed dividends on their preferred shares, typically in the range of 5-20% within a time frame of 5-10 years.

Closed-ended funds are the most frequently used because of their acceptance in the VC community.

Intended to create a set number of companies over a certain duration, providing investors with a more defined offering of what they are purchasing.

Initial funds tend to be small ($10M-20M) followed by funds of around $50M-100M. Once studios raise a third fund, they tend to be $100M-200M to be able to cover follow-ons.

Studios tend to raise every 3-4 years, which is shorter than the traditional VC cycle.

The Details

Single and dual-entity studio models involving a fund tend to also differ in their investment horizon and return timeline. We observed a split between open-ended and closed-ended funds within studios, generally seeing dual-entity structures using a closed-ended fund and single fund structures using an open-ended fund.

Open-Ended (Evergreen)

Studios like AlleyCorp, Polymath, Founders, and Rule 1 all chose to structure as evergreen funds or companies. This allow them to build and invest without rigid liquidation expectations and grants them the ability to return capital back into the organization for continued use. Studio growth can come from successful portfolio companies contributing additional capital raises into the pool of returns. In place of returns from a closed pool of investment, a number of studios offer investors guaranteed dividends on their preferred shares, typically in the range of 5-20%. An evergreen structure can be particularly beneficial for studios as it may facilitate the following:

- Allow LPs to join and exit as the studio matures
- Allow studios to modify operating budget needs based on

success or number of ventures in development

• Reduce the complexity associated with allocating management fees across multiple funds or ventures

• Allow the studio to change its venture building or investment thesis if necessary

• Allow studios to pursue opportunity areas that LPs of traditional closed-ended funds would not allow, like "sin industries"

While valuing the underlying illiquid assets of the studio can make LP management in open-ended funds a challenge, open-ended funds generally provide a degree of flexibility to studio leaders that close-ended funds cannot. When asked why their studio landed on an evergreen fund structure, Todd Ehrlich of Rule 1 shared the following:

> In a studio we are often starting from the idea stage, so having a 10 year closed-end structure adds unnecessary restrictions, which can result in strategic misalignment through forcing unsustainable growth rates or prematurely exiting opportunities. The result of the evergreen structure combined with a studio model provides the opportunity for both equity value creation along with dividend opportunities that can amplify returns on smaller capital investments, while also maintaining the ability to enjoy long-term returns from lasting companies rather than through exits alone. Most importantly, the majority of entrepreneurs we speak with are attracted to the model

> - Todd Ehrlich,
> Co-founder, CEO, and General Partner of Rule 1 Ventures

Given this, we wondered why open-ended funds are not the dominant structure in the venture studio landscape. Our hypothesis is that raising from LPs is generally more difficult with an open-ended structure. With startups, valuing investments is difficult and unreliable and time to liquidity is long. Being in a structure where fund upside is reinvested back into the studio can be hard for LPs to get behind, particularly when the comparison point is close-ended traditional VC funds. From our research, studios that were able to start with an evergreen fund did so because they worked with a small number of extremely patient LPs. And, once they had enough venture success or liquidity events, they were able to use the returns from companies to fuel studio growth. Not all studio leaders have access to patient LPs, particularly those who are new to the studio and investing landscape. Over time, we wonder if we will see more open-ended funds in the studio landscape. In 2021 Sequoia announced its first open-ended fund. Seeing a top-tier VC like Sequoia implement an open-ended model shocked the industry, and many wonder if it will start a trend towards more. The evergreen fund structure has worked well so far for Ulrik Trolle of Founders.

> A closed limited partnership is fair and square, because at the end of 10 years it is obvious how to share the pie between LPs and GPs. In an evergreen, however, there needs to be a longer-term, intergenerational trust between the parties. This is quite a leap of faith to take, especially for the GPs. But all the aspects making an evergreen 'sound business' convinced us that we had to take that leap. And thus far, after the first 10 years, we are convinced that we made the right choice.

> - Ulrik Trolle, Founder and Managing Partner at Founders

Close-Ended

Studios like Diagram and Atomic prefer close-ended funds or operating entities with a defined capital pool and time horizon.

Compared to open-ended funds, where the number of companies built with an investor's capital and the time to exit may be unclear, these funds are typically intended to create a set number of companies over a certain duration, providing investors with a more defined offering of what they are purchasing. Growth for studios with this fund structure often comes from success resulting in larger subsequent funds raised. This allows studios to increase their size, expand the number of companies created, and increase the amount available for follow-on investments. However, if separate funds are run in parallel, ongoing company support and allocation of management fees across companies can be more difficult.

An additional limitation of this structure is how much capital can be invested in follow-on rounds, and for how long (until Series B, C, etc.). To maintain their ownership in created companies, studios are forced to raise larger subsequent funds that can participate in follow-ons. These larger funds enable studios to invest longer in their companies, preventing their ownership from getting diluted and leading to larger exits. This is a trend we have seen occurring across the industry. The fund size we have observed is as follows: initial funds tend to be small ($10M-20M) followed by funds of around $50M-100M. Once studios raise a third fund, they tend to be $100M-200M to be able to cover follow-ons.

Even when studios can no longer invest in follow-ons due to fund size limitations, we heard studio leaders syndicating their pro-rata rights to their LPs. This enables LPs to continue receiving exposure into the portfolio and studios to capitalize on a greater portion of the pro-rata rights of their successful ventures. This model aligns closer with traditional VCs, and is thus likely more attractive to traditional LPs. However, from an operational perspective, ongoing company support and allocation of management fees across companies can be more difficult with separate funds.

Lastly, a consideration when structuring the fund is the horizon for the investments. In an ideal case, studio leaders could raise funds that would provide enough runway to reach the first round of exits. However, this tends to be a hard ask of LPs given that exits may take ~6-10 years. We observed studios raise funds every few years (3-4 years), a much shorter horizon than traditional VC funds. Studios can then use unrealized valuation trends and a few exits to justify the next fundraise.

Studio Financing
Section Summary

- All studios need to raise funds for their studio operations, regardless of how they structure or whether they choose to raise an investment fund.

- Studio leaders can find it challenging to convince investors because it is a new asset class and differs from traditional VC structures.

- Operating companies tend to maintain a small LP base, primarily from high net worth individuals and family offices.

- Studios raise ~$10M-20M from investors for the operating or holding company, with a few outlier studios raising $50M.

Characteristic of Studio Operating Entity	Target Investor Profile
Exposure to extremely early-stage venture development	Risk seeking
Holds founding equity in launched start-ups	Seeks direct exposure to portfolio companies and/or a successful venture builder
No clear exit path nor promised dividends from portfolio exits	Patient investors who do not need guaranteed returns for 5-7 years

The Details

Aside from the investment fund, studios need to raise funding for their own operations (below referred to as the operating entity). Because studios are a relatively new asset class, it can be harder for studio leaders to convince investors, who are used to VC structures, to invest in the operating entity. This challenge can be even more acute for studios operating in less mature entrepreneurial ecosystems where investors may be less familiar with the upsides of the studio model (Szigeti, 2019).

From our research, the following characteristics capture the target investor profile for a studio's operating entity:

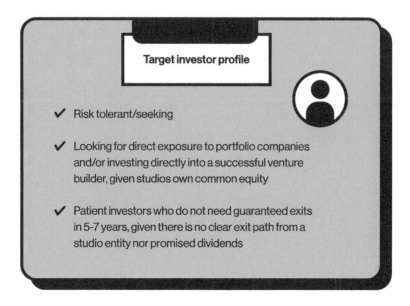

Target investor profile

✔ Risk tolerant/seeking

✔ Looking for direct exposure to portfolio companies and/or investing directly into a successful venture builder, given studios own common equity

✔ Patient investors who do not need guaranteed exits in 5-7 years, given there is no clear exit path from a studio entity nor promised dividends

As a result, operating companies tend to maintain a small LP base, primarily from high net worth individuals and family offices. These LPs tend to be more flexible and patient, which are critical traits given the nascency of the space. In terms of quantity, we generally saw studios raise ~$10M-20M from investors for the operating or holding company, with a few outlier studios raising $50M.

For studios structured as dual entities, leaders are raising capital for their operating company and investment fund from separate LP pools. Because studio investment funds are comparable to VC funds, they tend to have a larger and more diverse LP base compared to the operating entity. For example, one of the studios we spoke with had only 2 LPs for the studio itself but "dozens" for the fund.

As studios continue to mature and justify returns through their venture success and high levels of initial ownership, we expect increased participation from more traditional LPs at the operating company level.

Equity Ownership
Section Summary

▫ Equity ownership is variable by studios but the typical range is 25-40% ownership.

▫ Historically, many studios took majority ownership in their companies. This became a sticking point for investors or new employees. Studios have reacted by bringing down their founding stake and only 4 of 19 studios we spoke with take >50% common equity.

▫ Few studios have the capital available to fully participate in subsequent rounds, but studios with large fund sizes will maintain 20-35% ownership through Series A and B.

▫ Multiple studios did not have a standard equity stake within their portfolio. These are key factors that determined if the studio would take a higher equity stake:

☐ Studio-led idea generation

☐ First-time founder

☐ Founder is not contributing their own capital

☐ Founder is taking a cash salary

☐ Founder takes a non-CEO role

The Details

The number of companies that studios own is a critical driver of studio returns. Additionally, it also represents how much studios are willing to pay founders, which is one of the most important ways studios can attract entrepreneurs.

Equity splits between founders and studios are highly variable, however 25-40% studio ownership appears to be the most common range across studios. Few studios have the capital available to fully participate in subsequent rounds throughout the venture's life cycle, therefore many of them take initial ownership stake with the expectation it will decrease with future dilution. For some studios with large fund sizes, they will target an ownership range of ~20-35% through Series A and B.

We heard that many studios historically took majority ownership in their ventures (Szigeti, 2016). However, these studios struggled as a result. The higher equity stake prevented them from securing top founding talent and the non-traditional cap table confused potential VC investors. As a result, venture studios brought down equity stakes to a level accepted by entrepreneurs and investors alike, generally 25 40%. As an example, one studio we spoke with started by taking 70% ownership and realized they were unable to attract class A founders. They determined that the end result must be comparable to that if a founder started the company on their own, settling on at least 50% ownership to the founding team and employee option pool. Today, only 4 of 19 studios interviewed take majority ownership in ventures, citing they are "true founders." These studios tend to have more robust track records, ideation teams, and in-house support services to justify the high initial ownership share. Given equity splits are such a high priority issue, studio leaders need to be aware of and reactive to industry expectations.

Within individual studios, we saw a wide range of equity splits on a venture by venture basis. One studio we spoke with shared a range of 5-50% for equity founders can receive. Standard founder offerings outside of structured programs can be rare, complicating studio economics and negotiations. Studios often don't advertise EIR roles or compensation intentionally so that they can determine amounts on a case-by-case basis. There are some variables that affect founder/studio equity splits:

- Was the founder involved in idea generation?
- Are they a second time founder?
- Are they contributing any of their own capital?
- Are they taking salary or not?
- What role does the founder fill (CEO/CTO/CPO)?

These variables will dictate how much leverage the studio has in taking an increased ownership percentage at the outset.

Part 4:
Studio Model Deep Dive

Model Overview

To answer our second question, "What makes a venture studio financially viable?", we first needed to understand the studio financial model. As a result, we built out a high-level financial template informed by our research. The template is certainly simplified, but we used it to better understand decisions studios need to make. We hope it serves as a useful foundation for individuals looking to start a studio or for investors evaluating the space.

We start our analysis with a "base case." The base case represents the most simplistic single entity studio. The numbers are highly illustrative based on our assumptions.

From the base case, we introduce 4 independent levers that we identified as the most impactful to a studio's success:

 Revenue generation: billing back and corporate co-builds

 Raising a fund

 Equity ownership

 Exit outcomes: timing and distribution

The analysis and discussion below will dive into each of these levers individually. Our goal is not to focus on the absolute numbers, but rather the trends and directional impact of pulling on certain levers. We will compare results with each lever back to the base case. Finally, we will end the section with an "optimistic case." The optimistic case represents decisions we think a best-in-class studio would make. In the next sections, we will compare best-in-class VC returns to this optimistic case.

Of course, there are numerous assumptions that inform the model outside of these critical levers, such as funnel efficiency, process cost, etc. While these factors do vary across studios, we have assumed industry average estimates and focused the space on the most sensitive levers in the studio model.

Section Summary

We start with our base case and introduce each lever independently. We classify the impact as low, medium, and high based on the changes to cash balance, IRR, and MoM compared to the base case.

Highest impact levers are fundraising, lowering the equity stake, and timing of exits. Billing back is a medium impact lever.

			Year 10		
			Cash balance	**Realized IRR**	**Realized MoM**
Base Case			$90M	24%	9x
Lever	**Sub-lever**	**Impact**	**Cash balance**	**Realized IRR**	**Realized MoM**
Revenue generation	Billing back (post-validation)	MEDIUM	$95M	30%	14x
	Corporate co-builds	LOW	$92M	27%	11x
Raising a fund		HIGH	$98M studio $129M including fund returns	37% (studio) 15% (fund)	24x (studio) 4x (fund)
Equity ownership	Incremental 10% dilution each round	LOW	$75M	22%	7x
	Equity stake at 8% floor	HIGH	$1M	-20%	0.1x
Exit outcomes	Delayed exits	HIGH	$46M	10%	2.5x
	Timing (1 early exit)	MEDIUM	$110M	34%	19x
	Realistic distribution	MEDIUM	$199M	34%	19x

- The "best-in-class case" represents the decisions that we think a best in class studio would take. This includes:

  - Billing back after validation and working on corporate co-builds to generate revenue.

  - Having a closed-ended fund that will invest in 20% of spun out companies' follow-on rounds through Series B with a 2% management fee and 20% carry.

  - 1 early exit for $75M.

  - Realistic exit distribution with average value of $575M.

- In our best-in-class case, studios would achieve a 100% IRR and a 1000x+ MoM by year 10. By year 10, the first fund would be fully realized with an IRR of 26% and a MoM of 10x.

Base Case

The base case assumes the studio in the most simple version: no fund and no revenue generated, just simply building companies in exchange for founding shares. The base case assumes ideas are generated through a mix of internal efforts and a small number of EIRs. By year 10, the studio will be launching 7 new companies per year: 4 from internal-driven ideation efforts and 3 from EIRs. This is higher than most of the studios we spoke with (73% expect to launch <4 companies per year), but most studios now are younger than 10 years old. Our base case is projecting a future state. We assume that exits commence 5 years after spinning a company out, or 6 years from founding (see "Time to Raise" in section "Other Assumptions"). Lastly, the case assumes 30% of launched companies are projected to reach a successful exit (see section "Likelihood of Exit"). A successful exit is classified as an average value of $280M, which means 4% of exits reach unicorn status (see section "Distribution of Outcomes"). For a full description of the base case, please refer to the included model.

As with any business, reaching profitability and having a positive cash balance are key metrics to ensure viability. We mentioned above how raising capital can be challenging for venture studios given that they are a relatively new asset class for LPs. Thus, as we built the studio model, we focused on forecasting annual net income and cumulative cash balance to better understand how much funding the venture studio would need to be a sustainable business. For simplicity, we assume that net income is on a cash basis, so it also represents cash burn. Our projections for the base case are seen below in Exhibits 1 and 2.

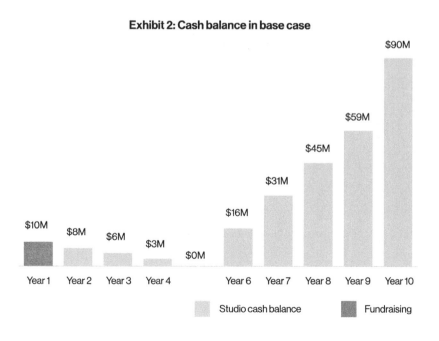

Exhibit 1: Net income in base case

$31.4M

$16.4M

$14.2M $14.1M $14.0M

($1.3M)   ($1.3M)

($2.1M)   ($2.3M)

($3.2M)

Year 1   Year 2   Year 3   Year 4   Year 5   Year 6   Year 7   Year 8   Year 9   Year 10

Exhibit 2: Cash balance in base case

$90M

$59M

$45M

$31M

$16M

$10M $8M $6M $3M $0M

Year 1   Year 2   Year 3   Year 4   Year 6   Year 7   Year 8   Year 9   Year 10

Studio cash balance   Fundraising

Because we assume the exits start materializing in year 6 and there is no source of revenue, the studio is running at a loss for 5 years. In the early years, the studio will burn from $1.3M per year (to launch 2 companies) to $3.2M in later years (to launch 5 companies). From our conversations, this is in line with the average studio operating budget of $2M. As shown in Exhibit 2 via the pink bar, the studio needs to raise ~$10M in cash to fund operations through year 5. However, once we hit year 6, the studio starts to see 1+ exit per year. Each exit brings in ~$22M per company, which enables the studio to run at a profit of ~$14M/year. Over 5 years of exits, the studio sees ~$132M in realized returns. This is over 10x what investors had put in, not to mention the potential millions sitting in unrealized returns. We assume that the profits from exits are reinvested back into the studio and its portfolio, but in reality, investors could receive distributions. If the studio were to pay out all profits as dividends to investors in year 10, that implies a ~24% realized IRR and 9x MoM.

Even in the base case, the strength of the studio model is clear. Once exits start rolling in, the cash generated can be enough to sustain studio operations. However, the model is not without its challenges. The primary challenge that studios face is cash flow. Studios are building companies, and while the value proposition is to accelerate company building, the entire process still takes a lot of time. Based on our assumptions, the studio burns cash through year 6, at which point exits begin. This challenge becomes even more pronounced if exits take longer to come in, or if the exit profile of investments do not meet the base case (see section "Dilution and Distribution of Outcomes"). Though it may sound like a small amount compared to venture investing, $10M may be challenging for studio management to secure given the industry's young age and potential LP hesitancy.

Revenue Generation

Assumptions for Billing Back

As mentioned in Part 3b, the most common approach we observed was to bill back for a portion of post-incorporation services. We saw substantial variance in when studios incorporated their portfolio companies, so we will demonstrate what billing back post-incorporation can look like, both after validation and MVP. The model assumes that any services post spin-out are billed at cost, meaning these services will have no net impact on net income. In the model we have assumed spin-out happens after the pre-Seed, which is 12 months from founding. While this is earlier than the studios we spoke with, we assumed 12 months to simplify the model mechanics and ensure all studio support is expensed in the first year of founding. In the case that spin-out occurs at Seed or Series A, then the model should be altered to show how studio support costs would extend over that multi-year period. If studios were to extend the length of their process/support, then they would also have to increase capacity to support companies. Thus, on a net basis, we believe the financials would be similar even with a Seed or Series A spin-out.

From our interviews, we observed that two cost measures mattered. First, the fully loaded cost to launch 1 company was heavily monitored. We generally saw studios putting in anywhere from an initial $250K-700K into each launched company, excluding formal investments. This included the cost of all the failed ideas that went through the funnel to get to the 1 successfully-launched company. In our model, we assume the distribution of idea and costs by stage below. We also assume additional post-incorporation recruiting and financial support for a total of $68K per incorporated idea. Thus, fully-loaded cost for a spun out idea ranges from $350K-415K in our model.

	# ideas	$K / stage
Ideation	25	5
Validation	3	50
MVP	1	150

The second cost measure that matters is how much studios can bill back. Practically, studios can only start billing their companies when those companies have funding. This means billing back usually does not start until at least the pre-Seed stage, when the company has spun out and received an initial check from the studio. At this point, a portion of the pre-Seed funding can be allocated to directly reimburse the studio for its services (i.e. if the studio provides $500K in pre-Seed funding but is owed $100K by the company, the company would net receive only $400K in funding). The amount of bill back is dependent on the margin/discount and the point of incorporation. Many studios that did bill back did so at cost, which we assume in the model. We assume that EIR-founded companies are billed back for all costs except EIR salary. The cost at validation and MVP are assumed to be slightly lower than for internally-founded companies, given that the EIR will be doing substantial work that the studio team would otherwise do. Below we have laid out the impact of billing back.

Financial Implications of Billing Back

Assuming incorporation comes after MVP development and studios bill for their post-incorporation services at cost, the studio only recoups $68K per company. As a result, the impact on the studio's cash balance is relatively small. The studio will need to raise $9M in total cash as compared to $10M in the base case, a difference of only $1M total. This is because most of the costs incurred happen during MVP development and testing. By not billing back the startups for those costs, the studio ends up completely eating the costs. In contrast, let's look at what happens if incorporation comes after validation (Exhibits 3 and 4). The studio can bill back each launched company for ~$200K, which is >3x what we saw above. This means in the early years, the studio sees $0.4M in revenue and grows to $1.5M in the out years. As a result, the studio would only have to raise $7M. This is a difference of $3M, representing a 35% reduction in total funds required by the studio. Post-incorporation bill back after validation makes a substantial difference in the studio's financial profile because the amount of costs incurred for MVP development and testing is disproportionately large (i.e. hiring external talent to build the product and advertising/testing expenses).

Exhibit 3: Net income with post-incorporation bill back after Validation

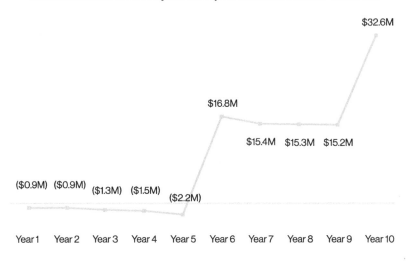

$32.6M

$16.8M

$15.4M $15.3M $15.2M

($0.9M) ($0.9M) ($1.3M) ($1.5M) ($2.2M)

Year 1   Year 2   Year 3   Year 4   Year 5   Year 6   Year 7   Year 8   Year 9   Year 10

Exhibit 4: Cash balance with post-incorporation bill back after Validation

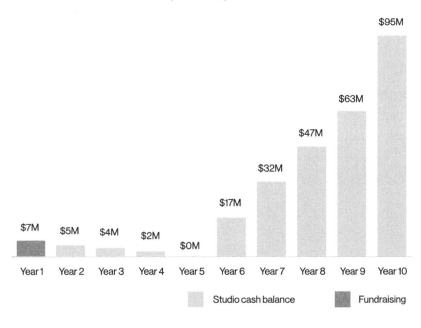

$95M

$63M

$47M

$32M

$17M

$7M $5M $4M $2M $0M

Year 1   Year 2   Year 3   Year 4   Year 5   Year 6   Year 7   Year 8   Year 9   Year 10

Studio cash balance   Fundraising

Now, the more aggressive approach, which is the rare situation where we observed studios billing back for pre-incorporation costs. If the studio did this at cost, the studio would only end up requiring $5M over 5 years. This is a whopping 50% in cumulative cash savings versus the base case.

Clearly, billing back can be a game-changer for studios. While the aggressive case we laid out is unlikely to materialize for most studios (as mentioned above, we observed very few studios billing back pre-incorporation, likely because it is a harder sell to entrepreneurs), billing back post-incorporation is a realistic option. Starting to bill back after validation makes a studio's financial profile significantly more palatable. Of course, the time of incorporation is not only a financial decision. As mentioned above, entrepreneurs may react differently to paying back pre-incorporation and post-incorporation costs. Studios that decide to incorporate after MVP may face more difficulty in billing back for those costs. Given all of this, new studios or those that are relatively cash strapped should 1) certainly consider billing back because even in the worst case, it results in some offset to expenses, and 2) should consider incorporating ideas after validation so costs can be recouped for the costly MVP development and testing period.

Assumptions for Corporate Co-Builds

Given the benefits of corporate co-builds (mentioned in Part 3b), we wanted to understand the revenue uplift that they provide to studios. To do so, there are four key assumptions required:

1) Margin charged for services: we assumed a 40% margin, which is in line with what we heard from studios.

2) Studio equity ownership at launch: Based on industry

practices, we assumed that the amount of equity which studios take is similar to that of internal ideas (30%).

3) Amount of studio time required to launch companies: We assumed that internally-launched ideas would require the same amount of time as corporate co-builds. While corporate co-builds may require more client management, their expertise is likely to counteract some of the team time required. We assume that studios will only start working with corporations in year 2, as the first year will be spent establishing studio operations and building processes. In year 2, the studio will co-launch with corporates one idea. This number will ramp to four by year 5 as the studio grows its capability and client pipeline.

4) Exit profile: For simplicity, we assume that the corporate co-builds see similar exits as internal efforts. We posit that corporate co-builds will see higher variance than internal efforts. As mentioned above, successes may result in larger and faster exits because the corporate partner would acquire the company. However, given the perceived strategic value of corporate co-builds, the flip side is that lower-performing companies would see a poorer exit path than internal builds. So, on a net basis, we assume the distribution of companies is similar whether internal or corporate-built.

Financial Implications for Corporate Co-Builds

Given these assumptions, corporate co-builds would reduce the studio's required cash to $9M from $10M in the base case, representing 17% cash savings. The studio would only burn up to $2.7M in a single year. Now, we have seen many studios combine both corporate co-building with billing back as dual revenue streams.

Adding post-incorporation bill back at validation would reduce studio cash requirements to $6M, with a max cash burn of $2.1M in a single year. Combining corporate co-builds with billing back results in 39% cash savings from the base case.

However, as discussed in Part 3a, there are many downsides of corporate co-builds. The main downside included in the model is the trade-off in team time required for corporate co-builds. This is showcased in Exhibit 5 below, where studio spin-outs approach zero in years 2 and 3 in order to make room for corporate co-builds. Given the downsides mentioned above, allocating team time entirely to co-builds can be costly for venture studios.

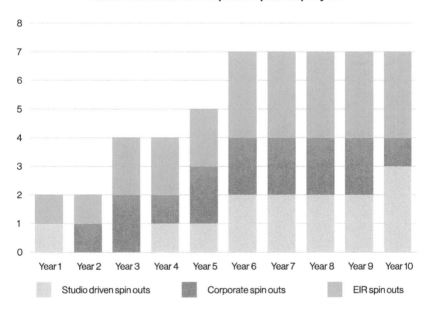

Exhibit 5: Number of companies spun out per year

Beyond the trade-off in team time, there is also the uncertainty in exit profile introduced via relationship with the corporate partner. Will the corporate partner provide guaranteed funding and a path to exit? What is the company's exit profile if the corporation is not interested in acquiring? These are questions that we are still understanding as an industry, and are therefore not captured in the numbers shown above.

While corporate co-builds are an attractive way to generate revenue and upside, the introduction of uncertainty can make them less attractive compared to internal company building. This explains why corporate co-builds only represent a portion of venture studio operations and almost never 100% of the business. For early studios, corporate co-builds can be a good path to pulling in revenue upfront. Over time, we recommend studios move to internal-driven launching efforts and away from corporate co-builds.

Raising a Fund

Assumptions

To understand the benefits and trade-offs of raising a fund, we have sensitized the model to the inclusion of a separate investing fund. The mechanics of the fund in the model is in line with the most common approaches discussed above. Specifically, the model includes the following elements:

☐ The structure assumed is a dual-entity structure.

☐ Assume there are four close-ended funds, each with a 3-year horizon. Though the vast majority of studios we spoke with raise funds a few years after inception, for simplicity we assume this studio begins with a fund.

☐ We assume fund size is in line with industry averages discussed above. The first fund is $45M, the second fund would be ~$90M, and the third and fourth funds would be ~$120M. This fund size implies the fund can invest in 20% of the preferred equity for every round from pre-Seed through Series B.

☐ Management fees are only over the horizon of the fund (3 years for each fund).

☐ The returns from the preferred equity shares go back to the

GPs/LPs of the fund and GPs receive 20% carry, where the GPs are likely the same as partners of the studio.

☐ The GP returns can be taken out by the partners or they can be reinvested into the studio. If they are reinvested, partners would receive equity in the holding company in exchange for the additional investment. As a result, GP returns can be a source of cash for the studio company, but not a source of income. The model doesn't assume a specific amount of cash is reinvested, but does show how the studio cash balance would be increased in a 100% reinvestment scenario.

☐ The management fees, assumed to be 2%, are a source of income to the studio.

☐ The studio receives a return from its founder shares in the form of income.

Financial Implications

Compared to the base case, if a studio were to raise the $45M, $90M, and $120M funds discussed above, the studio remains at or around break-even for 5 years before exits start coming in. At most, the studio would lose $1.5M in any single year (Exhibit 6). The management fees serve to offset most of the studio's expenses. The studio only needs an incremental $4M sitting at the operating company level to fund operations through year 6. And, once exits come in, studio cash balance would increase dramatically should GPs choose to reinvest their returns (Exhibit 7).

The fund return profile is strong. By year 11, the fund would be fully exited with an IRR of 17% and a MoM of 5.6x. However, when evaluating the performance of the studio asset class, it is important to look at the combination of fund and operating company. Having a fund brings the operating company IRR up to

37% and the MoM to 24x! The IRR grew by ~50% and the MoM nearly tripled. Having a fund makes the studio operating entity an even more attractive investment. Since the fund management fees are subsidizing studio operations, investors have to put in less capital for the same level of returns.

Exhibit 6: Net income after raising a fund

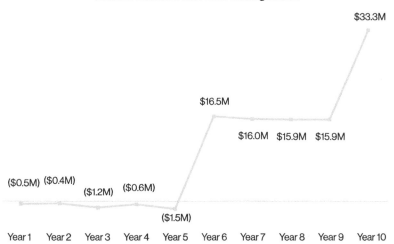

Exhibit 7: Studio cash balance after raising a fund

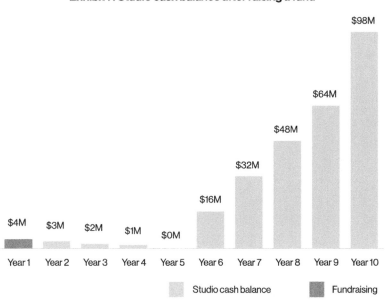

The studio cash flow profile looks even better with early exit assumptions. Assuming 1 early exit, the studio operating company would only need to raise a total of 24M over 6 years, and the fund would have a similar full-realized return of 5.2x MoM and 18% IRR. The operating company would now have a 50% IRR and a 57x MoM.

Thus, raising a fund is beneficial for studios not only because it brings in a source of revenue through management fees but also because GPs receive stellar returns from follow-on investments at cheap valuations. Because of these benefits, it is no surprise that we are seeing most studios move toward including an investing fund.

Equity Ownership

Since high levels of initial studio ownership is a key requirement in the economic success of the studio model, equity split and dilution are two highly important variables. Below we explore how different dilution scenarios impact studio returns. The below analysis is for our base case studio, which does not have a separate fund.

Dilution Sensitivities

To analyze the impact of dilution, the model includes a cap table for each round through Series D. The assumptions for the rounds are indicated below. Even though the studio starts out at 30% at the initial funding, it can get diluted to as low as 8% or lower by exit. The post-money valuation and round size for rounds up to Series B were assumed in line with industry data publicized by Wing VC (Wagner, 2015). For Series C and D, we assumed rounds were consistently at 20% of the TEV, as suggested by YC (Y Combinator, 2021). Compared to observed "hot" funding markets, our assumptions around valuation are likely conservative.

	Studio %	TEV	$ Raised
Pre-Seed	30%		
Seed	19%	$10	$2
Series A	15%	$50	$10
Series B	12%	$150	$30
Series C	9%	$250	$50
Series D	8%	$750	$150

To illustrate the model's sensitivity to dilution, we will increase the round size by 10% in each round while keeping the valuation constant. As a result, 0.7M more shares will be issued by Series D, which means each exit will only generate $19M for the studio as opposed to $22M in the base case. By year 10, this results in a $15M lower cash balance, which is a 17% reduction. Stepping up to a 20% increase in round size brings down each exit even further to $16M, which means by year 10 studio cash balance is $28M lower than the base case. This is a 31% reduction. The size of the studio's ownership stake is a critical driver of returns and one reason that studios end up raising funds

Ultimately, as the number of studios increases and competition for top tier EIRs and founders increases, studios will need to determine equity splits that are in line with industry averages and competitive relative to their own internal offering. This will be especially important for new studios and those without strong brand recognition. We anticipate increased competition will likely drive studio ownership shares down. However, necessary ownership percentages to justify the studio economic model will likely set the floor around 10%. The break-even point for a studio without a fund is 8%. At 8% and without a fund, studio ownership will be diluted down to 1% by Series D. At exit, that means each company only pulls in $3.6M for the studio. As indicated below in Exhibit 8, this is just enough to cover the studio's ongoing costs. Thus, at 10% founding equity, the studio will have enough money to operate, but not enough to provide returns to investors. This makes the model unsustainable.

Exhibit 8: Cash balance at equity floor

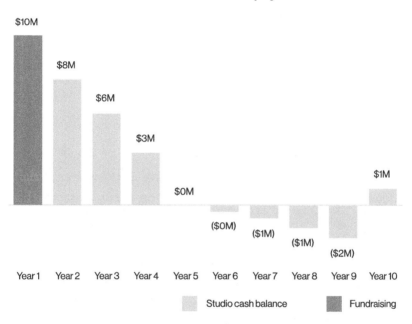

Top-tier studios and studios targeting "lower-tier" founders will likely still be able to maintain an ownership premium over industry average, and certainly above 10%.

Exit Outcomes

Studio exits are influenced largely by two factors: when they happen and how much they go for.

Timing of Exits

One of the key levers of returns is when exits will materialize. Studios experience substantial variance on a per company basis. From the studio leader interviews we conducted, we heard that they might see anywhere from 4 to 10 years for a company to exit. According to the National Venture Capital Association's 2021 Yearbook, the average age for a traditional VC investment to exit in 2020 was 6.3 years (NVCA Yearbook, 2021). Early fundraising data from studios show that they can raise rounds faster than traditional startups, so it would be reasonable to assume that studio-launched companies could also exit faster. To be conservative, we assume that the average time to exit is 6 years. However, we know that some studios might take longer to realize exits, so we sensitized the base case by assuming a longer time horizon of 8 years. The studio's illustrative net income and cash flow profile are below in Exhibits 9 and 10. With just 2 years extra in the average time to exit, we see a drastic impact on the studio's cash flow balance. Ending cash balance in year 10 produces a decrease in the base case of $90M to $46M. Additionally, the studio would have to raise $18M, an incremental $8M above the base case to fund the extra 2 years of operations before exits materialize.

Exhibit 9: Net income with delayed exits

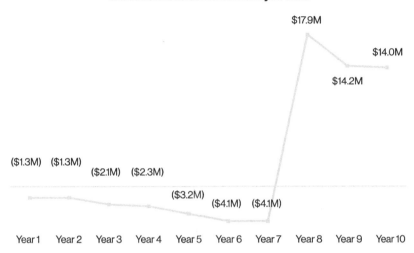

Exhibit 10: Cash balance with delayed exits

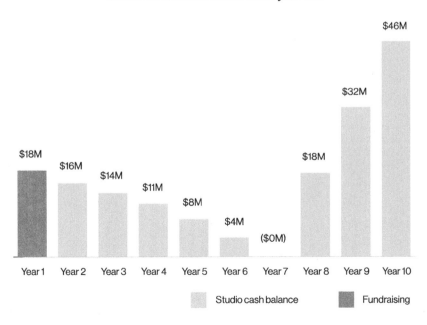

111

Timeline with delayed exits

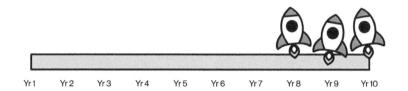

| Yr 1 | Yr 2 | Yr 3 | Yr 4 | Yr 5 | Yr 6 | Yr 7 | Yr 8 | Yr 9 | Yr 10 |

The time it takes for studio companies to exit is an important lever that can heavily influence the studio's return profile. To that end, studios can exercise some control over the exit timing. Specifically, early exits (i.e. 3 years post-launch instead of 6) can greatly benefit the studio by providing liquidity and reducing upfront cash needed. We sensitized the base case by assuming the studio would see 1 early exit of $75M at 4 years. The valuation is lower than what the studio would see from a typical Series B, as we assume that the studio is likely 1) selling off slightly worse performers and 2) may be a price taker. The studio's illustrative net income and cash flow profile are below in Exhibits 11 and 12.

Exhibit 11: Net income with early exit sensitivity

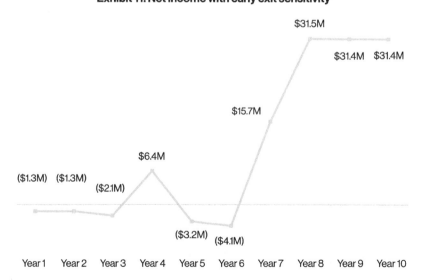

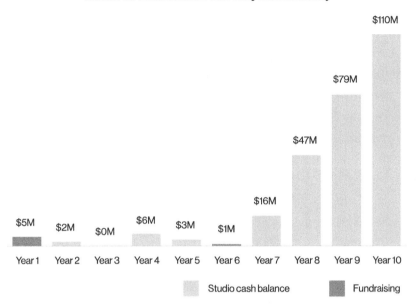

Exhibit 12: Cash balance with early exit sensitivity

$5M	$2M	$0M	$6M	$3M	$1M	$16M	$47M	$79M	$110M
Year 1	Year 2	Year 3	Year 4	Year 5	Year 6	Year 7	Year 8	Year 9	Year 10

Studio cash balance   Fundraising

Timeline with early exit

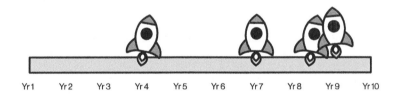

Yr1 Yr2 Yr3 Yr4 Yr5 Yr6 Yr7 Yr8 Yr9 Yr10

The early exit provides a ~$9M boost in income/cash to the studio in year 4. As a result, the studio only has to raise ~$5M up to year 5 to sustain operations (Exhibit 13). Then, the exit at $75M ends up funding year 5 of studio operations. In year 6, the studio needs to fundraise once more, for a small amount of $1M. This not only represents a 45% reduction in funds raised from the base case, but also provides an easier sequencing for studios for a few reasons. First, in the base case, the studio needs to raise a larger sum without having any historical successes. In contrast, with an early exit the studio raises only one-half of its total funds upfront and can raise the remainder once it has built a reputation. Second, in the base case, the studio is running at a loss every single year until the first exit. Thus, studio leaders need to always be cognizant of cash and having enough funding for the year after. The early exit provides studio leaders with some breathing room in year 4 so that they are not always burning through cash. An early exit means that the studio effectively gives up higher future returns for short-term liquidity.

Timeline with double early exits

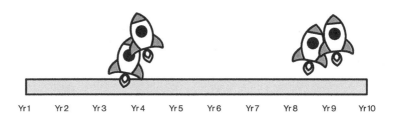

| Yr 1 | Yr 2 | Yr 3 | Yr 4 | Yr 5 | Yr 6 | Yr 7 | Yr 8 | Yr 9 | Yr 10 |

If we dive even further and assume 2 companies got early exits, the cash flow profile declines slightly. Because each incremental early exit provides ~$9M in cash to the studio, the studio would only need to raise $5M upfront (without the additional $1M). But, by year 10, the studio would actually have a lower cash balance by $10M+ (Exhibit 14). Taking a second early exit is leaving money on the table, which makes the studio slightly less attractive.

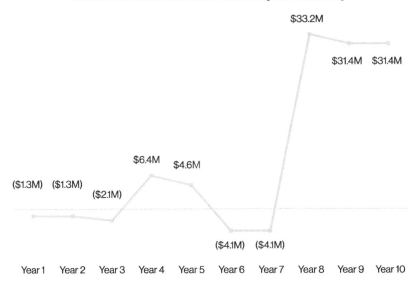

Exhibit 13: Net income with double early exit sensitivity

$33.2M

$31.4M $31.4M

$6.4M $4.6M

($1.3M) ($1.3M)

($2.1M)

($4.1M) ($4.1M)

Year 1 Year 2 Year 3 Year 4 Year 5 Year 6 Year 7 Year 8 Year 9 Year 10

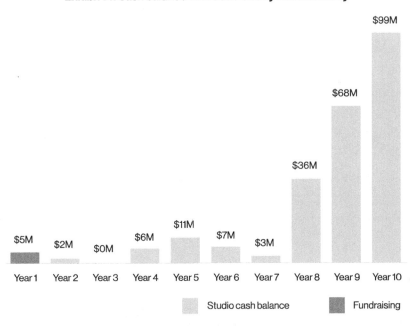

Exhibit 14: Cash balance with double early exit sensitivity

$99M

$68M

$36M

$11M

$5M $2M $0M $6M $7M $3M

Year 1 Year 2 Year 3 Year 4 Year 5 Year 6 Year 7 Year 8 Year 9 Year 10

Studio cash balance   Fundraising

Early exits can help mitigate the cash outflow challenge for studios. While studio leaders cannot guarantee when portfolio

115

companies will IPO or get acquired, they can secure an early exit through secondary sales to other VCs. Despite the benefits of secondary sales, we were surprised to hear that most studios we spoke with would rather hold equity until a true exit (M&A, IPO). The opposition against secondary sales is that it would "leave money on the table" and that they would be giving up their valuable equity for cheap and allowing other VCs to profit. As a result, the vast majority of studios we spoke with had not seen exits yet. While it is true that secondary sales do result in a smaller exit, as demonstrated above, it can be very helpful to ease fundraising needs for early studios by accelerating timeline to exit.

Additionally, even the "small exit" through a secondary sale represents a large return given the cheap founding equity studios receive. The early exit would provide $9M in return to the studio on a cost basis of virtually $0. To showcase the difference that early exits provide, one studio we spoke with had achieved 5 exits in the span of 10 years. This studio exited entirely through secondary sales. As a point of comparison, the next highest exit count was a studio that achieved 5 exits in 14 years, with an average time to liquidity of 8 years. Lastly, for geographies where entrepreneurship is less accepted, early exits can help accelerate growth of an entrepreneurial ecosystem and rapidly build a network of successful CEOs. These can all be tapped into for future builds (Szigeti, 2019). Newly-founded studios should highly consider implementing secondary sales in the early years to line up successes that ease later fundraising.

Distribution of Exits

One bet of the studio model is that portfolio companies will be able to achieve strong exits. Given that most studios we spoke with are young, the industry does not yet have enough significant data around valuation at exit. However, a few studios shared that exits around $50M were expected, with a few in the portfolio optimistically reaching $1B+. From publicly-available data on studio exits, we generally see exit values of <$1B. As examples, Gilt Groupe sold at $250M, Business Insider sold at $500M, and Dialogue IPO'd at $779M.

While success stories like Snowflake (valuation of ~$33B) are highly publicized, we believe they are anomalies. From GSSN's data, we see that best-in-class studios have been able to create unicorns at a rate of >4% (The Rise of Startup Studios, 2020). Idealab has specifically seen 5% of their launched companies become unicorns (Disrupting the Venture Landscape, 2020). For the purposes of the base case, we modeled that ~30% of launched companies will have a successful exit (see section "Likelihood of Exit"). The distribution of successful exits has 40% exiting at <$50M and ~4% exiting at $1B+. In total, 20% of companies are generating ~70%+ of the return. On a portfolio of 100 launched companies, 30 would have exits. Of those 30, 1 would be a unicorn.

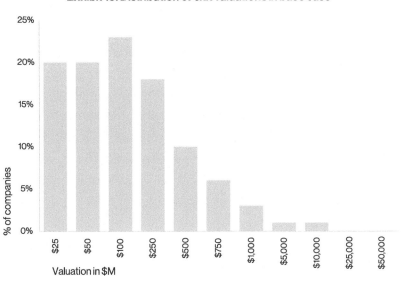

Exhibit 15: Distribution of exit valuations in base case

Exhibit 16: Return composition in base case

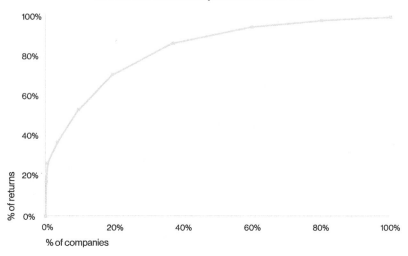

This type of distribution might sound familiar. In venture capital it is referred to as the "power law," when a large percentage of the returns come from a small percentage of the investments. Due to the high-risk nature of early stage startup investments, VCs see companies at extremes. A small minority of companies end up being huge wins, while the rest tend to underperform. Thus, VCs end up playing a numbers game, trying to make the most investments so that a few will be the decacorns that make the fund. Because studios are playing in a similar company stage, we thought it was reasonable for the power law to still apply. As mentioned in the base case above, this results in the studio burning $22M in total cash where each exit results in $22M pre-tax return from founding shares and $14M annual profit. In the base case, the studio operating company has a return of 9x MoM and 24% IRR, assuming dividends are paid out in year 10 (without a fund). But, given the importance of exits to the studio model, we wanted to sensitize our case to different types of outcomes.

First, we wondered how a more optimistic outcome distribution would impact the model. From our conversations, multiple studios stated that having a company reach unicorn status was their "north star." Keeping this in mind, having only 1-2 companies reach unicorn status on a portfolio of 100 could be a little low. So, we built an optimistic case where triple the number of companies in the portfolio would reach unicorn status and only 25% would exit at valuations <$50M. The average exit valuation in the optimistic case was ~$575M, about 2x the conservative case. The income and cash profile are included below in Exhibits 17 and 18. Because the profile of exits only becomes relevant at year 6, the funds the studio has to raise is still $10M (same as the base case).

However, the increase in cash is drastic after year 6, when exits start rolling in. By year 10, under these optimistic assumptions, the studio builds up $199M in cash. This is nearly $100M above the base case! In a single year, the studio will start throwing off ~$32M-68M in profit. Studios able to achieve this level of exits are not only more sustainable, but also much more attractive for investors. The operating company would have a MoM of 19x and IRR of 34%. They can easily afford to pay dividends to operating entity investors while simultaneously growing company building operations. We imagine that this exit profile is being realized by a subset of industry-leading studios.

Exhibit 17: Net income in realistic exit distribution

| | | | | | | | | | $67.8M |

$34.5M

$32.3M $32.3M $32.2M

($1.3M) ($1.3M)

($2.1M) ($2.3M)
($3.2M)

Year 1   Year 2   Year 3   Year 4   Year 5   Year 6   Year 7   Year 8   Year 9   Year 10

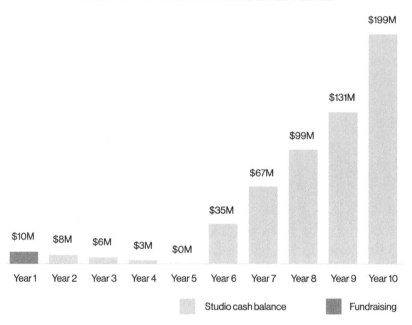

Lastly, what if the return profile of studios was different? One of the core ideas behind studios is that they result in more de-risked and stable performing companies. As a result, it may be the case that returns from companies are also consistent. The average exit would be lower without the power law at play, but there would not be a tail of exits on either the high or low end. It remains to be seen whether studios can achieve this level of consistency, but we wondered if the venture studio model would still be viable in this case. So, we analyzed a set of outcomes where the distribution of exits is more even (Exhibits 19 and 20). We assumed that 30% of companies exit at less than $50M, 35% exit at $100M and the remaining 35% exit at $250M. The average company exit would be $138M, approximately half of the realistic case. The lower valuation at exit results in the studio accumulating significantly lower cash by year 10. The studio would only accumulate $37M as opposed to $90M in the base case. However, the exits are sufficient when the profit is enough to fund studio operations and result in $5-14M in annual profit. Even without the power law, studios would still be financially viable.

Exhibit 19: Net income in even exit distribution

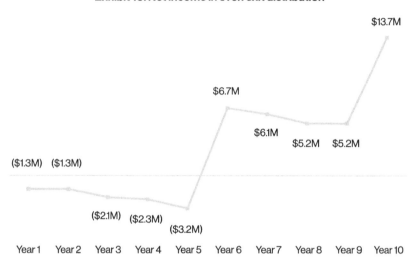

Exhibit 20: Cash balance in even exit distribution

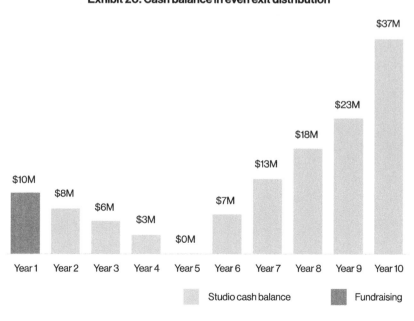

Similar to timing of exits, studios do not have control over the distribution of outcomes. The terms of valuation may be set by sellers and are often determined by market dynamics. However, studio leaders need to be aware of how valuations at exit can impact the studio's cash needs and attractiveness to investors.

Likelihood of Exit

The last aspect of distribution is the likelihood of a successful exit. We alluded to it in the process portion of Part 3, but one attractive aspect of the studio model is that launched companies have a higher likelihood of success than traditionally launched start-ups. According to GSSN, 60% of studio-founded companies reach Series A. In the same report, GSSN highlights that Idealab, one of the original venture studios, has seen 35% of its companies exit through an IPO or acquisition (Disrupting the Venture Landscape, 2020). So, in the studio model, we assume that 60% of launched companies make it to Series A and ~30% make it to a successful exit. For the models purposes, we define a successful exit as an exit after Series D, equal to $280M in the conservative case discussed above.

"Best-in-Class" Case

Given all of the levers described, we wanted to pull together a "best-in-class" case representing a venture studio that integrates the best practices we described above. The "best-in-class" case assumes the following:

Revenue Generation

To prevent an extended cash flow gap, the studio will generate revenue through two common ways. First, it will bill back spun out companies for all costs incurred post-incorporation, where incorporation is after validation. Second, the studio works on corporate co-builds to generate revenue

Raising a Fund

The studio will have a closed-ended fund in a dual-entity structure. Given the challenges of securing LPs who are comfortable with open-ended funds, we believe most studios will continue to raise closed-ended funds. To prevent complications between the fund and the studio, we opt for a dual-entity structure. The fund will invest in 20% of spun out companies' follow-on rounds through the Series B with a 2% management fee and 20% carry. As raising a fund becomes increasingly common, we assume that the studio starts with a fund at inception.

Exit Outcomes

At 4 years post-launch, studio leadership will intentionally decide to have 1 early exit for $75M. Additionally, we assume the realistic distribution of exits. The distribution follows the power law with an average exit size of $575M.

With these assumptions and seen below in Exhibits 21 and 22, the studio would be very close to profitability through year 6. In aggregate, the studio would only have to raise a small $200K in the first year. Because of the revenue streams from billing back and corporate co-builds, one early exit is sufficient to carry the studio's operations through year 6. In year 7, we start to see the rest of the portfolio exiting, which builds up the cash balance to ~$255M by year 10!

Given the low capital required, investors in the studio operating company would be well in the money. Assuming all profits were theoretically distributed, realized IRR would be 100% and MoM would be >1000x! The studio could easily pay dividends and return investor capital from the operating company, while still maintaining enough cash to operate for the future.

Exhibit 21: Net income in "best-in-class" case

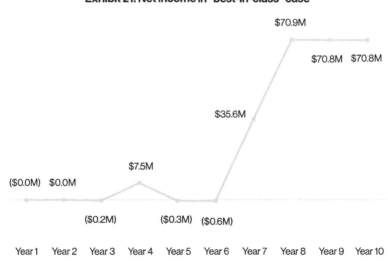

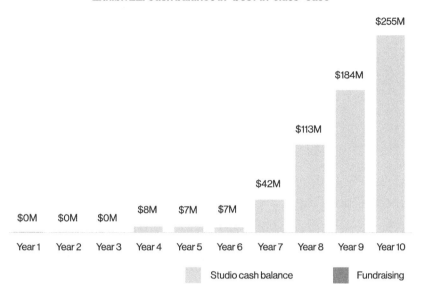

Exhibit 22: Cash balance in "best-in-class" case

Studio cash balance · Fundraising

From a fund perspective, the four funds would be $45M, $89M, $117M, and $117M, each with 3 year horizons. The fund's returns would result in $91M of additional cash available to the studio by year 10. The fund would be fully exited in year 10 with a MoM of 10x and realized gross IRR of 26%. GPs of the fund would see $28M in aggregate return by year 10. This "best-in-class" studio has comparable returns to a top-tier VC.

This is a drastically different profile than the base case. The levers indicated above go a long way to improve the return profile of studios. Though we started with a compelling financial model in the base case, the "best-in-class" case is even more compelling for investors and studio partners (fund GPs) alike.

Of course, the model is built on several assumptions and there is risk that certain areas, such as corporate co-builds, might not materialize as projected. We have summarized a few remaining assumptions below.

Other Assumptions

Time to Raise

Given the cash flow challenge that venture studios face, the time it takes for startups to raise funding is a critical lever in financial sustainability.

Part of the value of venture studios is that upfront testing and work not only leads to a higher chance of success, but also faster times to exit. GSSN found that the time from zero to Seed for a studio was 11 months, as compared to 36 months for a traditional startup. The time from Seed to Series A was for a studio was 14.5 months, compared to 20 months for a traditional startup (Disrupting the Venture Landscape, 2020). The faster studio companies can raise additional funding rounds, realize exits through secondary equity sales, or theoretically IPO. In the model template, we have included assumptions around time to raise each successive round, as well as time to exit. We assume that all companies have the same timeline to raise and exit, but in reality, there would be a distribution of outcomes.

Source of Ideas

We see that studios tend to generate ideas through the three main paths described in Part 3: 1) structured founder programs; 2) limited full-time positions; and 3) assigning founders to developed concepts.

For simplicity, we have included a toggle in our model for whether EIRs are leveraged as a source of ideas or not. Key levers around EIRs are whether they take cash compensation, how many succeed in launching a business, and how long it takes for ideas to launch. The first lever (cash compensation) is discussed in detail above. The second lever, how many succeed in launching a business, varied substantially across the studios. One studio quoted a success rate of 3 out of 50 EIRs in their 3-month program. Another studio claimed to select 1-4 EIRs from a pool of 200, and all would result in launched companies. Studio programs tend to go between 3-6 months on average.

We have also provided flexibility to vary the amount of costs attributable to EIR-led ideas. We assumed that EIRs draw a studio-paid salary while they are working on their idea but do not incur any studio driven ideation costs, and only incur a portion of costs during validation and MVP design. These costs may include paying for engineering, FB ads, etc.

While there are financial tradeoffs to each of these paths, there is no clear superior path. It is completely dependent on the studio's philosophy and the exact inputted assumptions. Thus, we have not included model outputs here and recommend leaders play around with the assumptions.

Team Constraints

Even with entrepreneur-led ideas, resources are needed to drive the process. For internal ideas, team members need to work through customer validation and prototyping. Thus, understanding how many ideas any single team member can manage at a single point in time is critical for studio founders. From the studios we spoke with, 1-3 ideas per ideating team member is standard.

Process

We assume that the process takes 12 months end to end, after which the company is spun out from the studio. As mentioned above, the time to launch was highly variable, with studios ranging from 6-18 months. For simplicity, we assumed 12 months as a median in terms of model mechanics.

Lastly, the efficiency of ideas through the funnel are important levers and the model has functionality for each of these to be varied. The exact mechanics and impact of changing these areas are described in Part 3.

Part 5: Conclusion

In writing this book, we set out to answer a number of key questions about venture studios. Below, we summarize our answers to each of them.

 What are the best ways to design and run venture studios?

We identified key levers and decision points that help determine an optimal way for leaders to design and run their studio. This includes revenue generating mechanisms, fund structures, EIR programs, and founder/studio equity splits. Ultimately, each of these levers and decisions has their own set of pros and cons, and every studio should determine which choices best fit their areas of expertise and goals. We recommend studio leaders consult our tear sheet to review these decision points and choices.

What makes a venture studio financially viable?

In order to understand bare minimum performance for studio viability, we also modeled various performance outcomes. With conservative exit valuation estimates, a studio needs at least a 10% equity stake in founded companies in order to cover ongoing costs. The comparable valuation "floor" is approximately $60M. If companies are exiting on average at $60M, the studio will be at breakeven in perpetuity.

What we really wanted to ultimately know is, "are venture studios an appealing asset class for those looking to enter the space?" And the answer appears to be, "yes, depending on who you are."

How successful is the venture studio industry overall?

Based on our research, the success of the venture

studio asset class as a whole is still murky, but it appears to be both widely acknowledged and lucrative for successful, high-performing studios. Studios like High Alpha, Atomic, and Founders have been able to raise significant subsequent capital, implying that they have demonstrated success to their LPs. And a number of studios have produced startups valued over $500M. Reports of high unrealized returns and well-publicized exits (Hims, Snowflake, MongoDB) prove that the asset class can provide outsized returns relative to VC. However, widespread data on actual studio performance remains limited.

We modeled out various scenarios for studio performance to understand what success for a single given studio would look like. In our "best-in-class" scenario, with an average company exit valuation of $575M (3% reaching unicorn status) and revenue support from billing back and corporate co-builds, a studio's realized IRR (just the operating company) would be 100% and MoM would be 1000x+. For the investing fund, the fully exited fund in year 13 would have an IRR of 26% and a MoM of 10x. For comparison, venture capital funds from 2010-2016 had an average IRR of 21.9%, with the top quartile coming in at 25.6% (Cambridge Associates, 2019). The S&P was 12.2% over the same time period. The studio fund on its own is a match for venture capital, not to mention the additional return that investors see at the operating company level. There are of course many assumptions going into our model, and we've highlighted how the returns could change depending on the fund size, equity ownership, and timing of exit. Regardless, the combination of operating company returns and fund returns indicate that studios can be a substantially higher returning asset class than VC.

In addition to looking at venture studio performance, we also wanted to look at how many studios try and fail. The best estimates on studio survival rate came from Enhance Ventures. Alper Celen, founding partner at Enhance, indicated that their survey of over 700 venture studios revealed that ~18 studios closed shop in the last two years. This resulted in an annual studio failure rate of around 1.3%. However, he indicated that this is likely an under-estimate, as many studios are still too young to fail and a large portion of them are likely still operable but not delivering sustainable returns to investors. Unfortunately, there is limited data on the average lifespan of a venture studio. The data that is available on studios tends to face significant survivorship bias. Therefore, limited performance data from failed studios means that many public reports on studio performance are likely biased upward when compared to the real performance of the asset class as a whole.

Implications for Stakeholders

We have covered a substantial amount of information in this book. Stepping back from the details, we wanted to end with our thoughts on where the studio model is going and what it means for each of the key stakeholders: investors, studio founders, and entrepreneurs.

For Investors

Venture studios are an interesting way to diversify your portfolio while still participating in the startup ecosystem. The economic model of studios proves that you can see large returns with enough capital and sustained high ownership, whether investors sit at the operating company or the fund. They also appear to be successful in their primary selling point of de-risking startup creation and shortening the timeline to create and scale early ventures relative to non-studio startups. It is still to be seen whether studios can generate more consistent returns than VC, a class where a few outsized winners make the entire fund. When asked about this with regards to his studio, Francois Lafortune of Diagram Ventures shared the following:

Our best performing portfolio companies will generate out-sized, fund-returning outcomes. However, by having a much higher 'batting average' and a better overall portfolio distribution (less zeros), it makes us less reliant on a signal monster winner. We think that translates into better risk-adjusted returns for both investors and founders partnering with us.

- Francois Lafortune, CEO of Diagram Ventures

Studios able to raise a significant amount of patient capital at the outset have also had the luxury of being able to take more bets. This is a privilege that other upstart studios may not have, and it increases odds for success.

If the broad venture market remains healthy, then we expect investment in venture studios to continue its rapid pace with more traditional LPs beginning to invest with established studios. More risk-averse investors may choose to put their money in associated studio investment funds or wait until new studios see success with initial cohorts. However, given the extremely small number of established studios, investors looking to enter the asset class may be forced to take on increased risk investing in new or developing studios. Multiple studio leaders we spoke with mentioned fund-raising being a challenge. Over time, as LPs become more comfortable with the space, we hope that this will no longer be an issue.

For New Studio Founders

Operating a venture studio is no small feat. Unlike with traditional fund management, venture studios require operators to personally navigate all the roadblocks and headaches associated with startups. They must come up with new venture concepts and be diligent in moving them forward. Studio founders should ideally have no shortage of ideas, and many are drawn to the model because they have more ideas than they can build themselves. And for those who can execute on the model successfully, the economic returns can be abnormally lucrative.

As we have alluded to throughout this book, one of the biggest challenges for starting and managing a studio is funding. Many of the established studios that we spoke with, like High Alpha, PSL, and Atomic, make the studio model look attractive and "easy," so to speak. However, that does not capture the stress and sweat that is required from each of these leaders to raise the sufficient funding to get their studio off the ground. Though studios aim to streamline their innovation process as much as possible, building companies is not cheap! If studio leaders cannot secure funding at founding, they will never be able to reap the benefits of the model.

In our research, we enumerated a few ways that studio leaders today are solving the cash flow issue. This includes raising a substantial amount of funding upfront from patient LPs, generating revenue through bill back or corporate co-builds, or selling stakes early through secondary sales. The second paths of income generation, while common now, pose challenges in that they are contrary to the goal and mission of founding companies and supporting them until exit. We believe that with time, as the model becomes more accepted in traditional investing circles, the first path will become easier for leaders. For leaders who want to start a studio, ensuring they have enough cash for a multi-year runway is the most important key to success.

While many studios believe they have their own "secret sauce" to ideation, process, and founder recruitment, we found that studios we interviewed mostly shared the same fundamental process. It is unclear whether the nuances in process lead to differentiated returns. As more studios crowd the space, internal process may become an important competitive differentiator. Yet despite this, we have found that studio leaders are broadly willing to share learnings across those areas with their peers in the industry. The space is still quite new, and many studio partners have expressed a strong belief that a rising tide lifts all ships.

Aside from the above, studio leaders face key decision points around structure, founder programs, and industry focus, among others. We see successful studios across many of these variables: open-ended versus closed-ended fund, dual-entity versus single-fund structure, structured founder program versus assigning founders to ideas. There is no superior path or choice. It all depends on the studio's philosophy, surrounding environment, and fundraising constraints.

For Entrepreneurs Looking to Work with Studios

While we constructed this book from the perspective of studios and their investors, the entrepreneur is another party critical for studio success.

For entrepreneurs, studios can be an excellent option if you have an ambitious mindset but don't have a clear idea of what you want to build. Having partners and structure around the ideation process can be quite helpful, and having the opportunity to join an already de-risked idea is even more appealing to some. Studios highlight how costly not having an idea can be, and they may even take majority ownership in these instances. The sacrifice of initial founding shares may be felt particularly hard down the road, especially with the frequency of company pivots in early stages. However, if your alternative was not being able to start a company at all, this may be a more than acceptable price to pay.

For a number of founders or repeat entrepreneurs, having a "co-founder" to handle back-end administrative needs and assist with funding and recruiting is worth the hefty price tag. Founders may think of studios as their non-technical co-founders, and give them co-founder level shares, but these services are paid for in pre-Seed and often cease to be available through the company's life. Studios provide significantly more value than a single non-technical co-founder, but their assistance often doesn't last forever. Therein lies the tradeoff. Founders should determine if they need the early support and expertise in order create a viable business, otherwise they may be able to receive similar support from more traditional venture capital sources at a less dilutive cost.

Studios can provide significant expertise in early venture development, however you should conduct careful diligence on the studio and its partners before joining. Determine what assistance they will provide, the quality of their services, how closely they work with their ventures, and how long they will continue to support you after your company spins out and continues to grow.

Studios and Innovation

To many, the mystique and appeal of studios lies in their unique ability to innovate at scale. In reality, studios tend to be a story of economic ownership levels, not superior ideation. Studios themselves don't necessarily need to be the most "innovative" players in the venture ecosystem, and that is good because the studio model has built-in, inherent limits to innovation. Compared to traditional venture capital, which reviews ideas from entrepreneurs around the world, studios generally only have their own staff and a handful of EIRs to pull ideas from. In addition, creating disruptive technology and innovating at the tech frontier can be extremely time-consuming and costly. This simply doesn't fit with the studio's economic model of failing fast and minimizing cost on failed ideas to preserve runway.

For this reason, studios typically design within the tech frontier and apply existing business models or solutions from other industries to the problem area they are exploring. The high-profile success stories originating from studios may prove this isn't that big of a problem after all. And studios unable to generate unicorn-type exits may be just fine as well. High initial ownership at a low cost means that exits of only $50M or $100M may still generate 50x or 100x returns. Studios appear to be proving the theory that strong execution may be far more important than truly game-changing ideas, and their economic design and areas of focus support that flexibility as well.

From our research, we have seen that 1) a number of studios have focused around B2B SaaS and 2) the process of venture studios tends to be centered around creating businesses that serve niche needs. As studios scale and more venture studios enter the industry focusing on similar industries and sub-sectors, it may become harder to generate ideas that suit the venture studio model, This is particularly due to how wide the initial idea funnel needs to be to result in one launched company.

We believe that this "limit" is a long way away. Entrepreneurs haven't had significant issues to date generating or receiving funding for their ideas. Additionally, studios are not "flooding" the market with net new ideas. Many studio entrepreneurs are individuals who would start their own business outside of the studio anyway. However, if we do reach such a limit, we expect to see consolidation in the studio landscape in favor of those established studios that have strong connections in the local entrepreneurial environment.

Industry's Path Forward

We have seen rapid studio growth over the last decade, but where does the asset class go from here? While we don't know the success rate of studios themselves, we do know the return potential for the studios that are successful. And this prospect is creating a mini "gold rush" as new studio creation continues to rapidly rise and new investors look to join in on the action. As the asset class expands, it will be interesting to see where new studios originate from. We hypothesize there are a few potential paths for expansion for the landscape.

First, we imagine that traditional venture capital firms will continue to expand their interest in studios and begin building studios of their own. We think it is likely that VC firms form studios of their own to work with high-potential founders or build ideas. These funds have the added advantage of leveraging existing capital to fund follow-ons. As VC firms move "downstream" and studios raise funds to move "upstream," we anticipate increased competition to attract founders and startup leaders. As studios try to attract best-in-class founders, we may see equity splits move in favor of the founder and push the VC/studio closer to the "equity floor" discussed above. We will also be curious to see if traditional VC firms and studios find innovative ways to develop symbiotic partnerships.

Second, high-profile entrepreneurs who have found success starting studios can pave the way for other top-tier entrepreneurs and operators to start studios of their own. Given the frequency that we observed the entrepreneurial origin story (12 of the 19 studios we spoke with), we believe this path will continue to be a strong source of studio growth. This should increase the amount of quality investment targets for LPs. However, not all new studios will be high quality and with the good comes the bad. More market entrants will mean a significant increase in low quality, high-risk studios entering the market. Analogous to new technology, we believe that venture studios as an asset class are going through a hype cycle. We have seen an "innovation trigger" and have been slowly climbing to the "peak of inflated expectations."

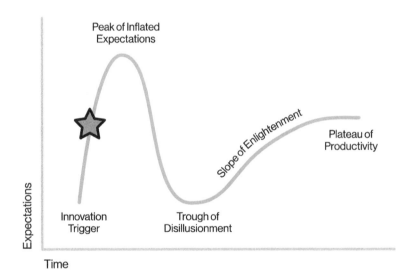

Until the peak, we expect that the demand for exposure from LPs will outpace studio creation and make fundraising feasible for non-premiere studio founders as well. As the asset class evolves and LPs become more familiar with the mechanics, we will get to the mature stages of the cycle. LPs will be able to distinguish the strongest studio founders and cater their investment to risk appetite. LPs who are low risk can double down on proven studio founders, whereas LPs who want a higher risk profile can provide investments to new studios at attractive terms. For the most part, we imagine that established studios with strong track records will continue to take on more capital as premier investment targets, with some ongoing studio creation and failure occurring each year.

As more capital flows into this asset class, the question then becomes, "how far can the studio model stretch? Is there a natural limit to studio portfolio size?"

Studios can continue to scale and deploy capital by increasing follow-on investment in successful studio companies and expanding studio operations (i.e. launching more companies). There should generally be enough investable companies created by studios to deploy this capital, as many successful studios have a number of launched companies progressing toward later stage rounds. As a result, we do not believe follow-on investments will pose any limitation to the studio model. However, we believe there are a number of constraints and incentives that make dramatic scaling of operations difficult. From an economic perspective, the preferred path for many scaling studios would be to use additional capital to scale company-building operations. This would allow the studio to take founder-level equity in significantly more ventures, increasing the number of bets a studio can take on developing a winner. However, the studio model requires high-touch, high-involvement participation from studio personnel and expert studio partners to justify co-founder equity shares. To grow the number of ventures launched and managed would require meaningfully expanding studio partnerships, an unlikely outcome since partners may be hesitant to give up portions of their carry and studio ownership. Additionally, scaling the team size can also present significant managerial challenges that lead to less rapid ideation and decision-making capabilities. For these reasons, many studio founders may make the philosophical choice to keep studio teams small, thus imposing a natural limitation on the number of ideas a single studio can manage.

As a result, we wonder if we might see established studios use their funds to Seed new studios in due time. Given the attractive financial profile of fully-funded studios, it seems a no-brainer that established studios who keep raising larger funds could allocate some of that capital to new studio leaders, especially as they hit constraints around how many ideas their own team can support.

All of these predictions point to substantial growth in the asset class, whether from VCs, serial entrepreneurs, or experienced studios seeding new ones. Venture studios are picking up steam, and we don't expect the train to stop any time soon. When executed correctly, we believe studios to be a highly lucrative model with staying power in the startup ecosystem.

Acknowledgements

We would love to give a special thanks to the following studio leaders who generously contributed their time and insights to the development of this project.

Wendy Tsu	AlleyCorp	Blake Koriath	High Alpha
Jordan Kong	Atomic	Matt Armstead	Horizon Two Labs
Keith Lindner	Coplex	Evan Cohen	Human Ventures
Miles Dotson	Devland		
Francois Lafortune	Diagram	Meshal Alshammari Abdulrahman Alzaid Hamad Almuqbel	Lean Node
Quentin Nickmans Sarah Barron	eFounders		
Alper Celen	Enhance Ventures	Marc Zapp	Next Big Thing
Roberto Sanabria	Expa	Greg Gottesman	Pioneer Square Labs
Jose Marin	FJ Labs	Wenyi Cai	Polymath
Ulrik Trolle	Founders	Matt Glickman	Promise
Prathna Ramesh	FutureSight	Brent McCrossen	Revelry
Regan Smith	GSSN	Todd Ehrlich	Rule 1 Ventures

We would also like to thank Prof. Josh Lerner, Prof. Ilya Strebulaev, Prof. Jeffrey Seglin, Scott Kupor, and Rob Siegel, all of whom shared their knowledge with us and provided valuable comments as we compiled our findings.

Lastly, a special thanks to our friends and colleagues who helped us polish this book into the version you're reading today.

About the Authors

Mitchel Peterman

Mitchel Peterman is an MBA graduate from the Stanford Graduate School of Business and MPA graduate from the Harvard Kennedy School.

Mitchel has worked with multiple startups in both the criminal justice and digital health spaces, serving a variety of leadership roles including strategic operations, marketing and communications, and business development. His love of entrepreneurship and curiosity about startup creation drew him to working with venture studios, and he has worked with early studios to develop internal operations and business design efforts. Mitchel is passionate about exploring ways that public policy can better support the development of social impact ventures, with a specific interest in criminal justice, healthcare, and media.

A proud born-and-raised Wisconsinite, Mitchel loves hiking, cheese curds, and the Green Bay Packers. When not writing about venture studios, he can be found spending time out on the lake, making homemade pasta, or poorly attempting sketch comedy.

Mitchel graduated Magna Cum Laude from Northwestern University. He holds a Bachelor of Science in journalism from the Medill School of Journalism and a Bachelor of Arts in Economics.

Shilpa Kannan

Shilpa Kannan is an MBA graduate from the Stanford Graduate School of Business. She is currently working as a Product Manager at Amazon.

Shilpa started her career in private equity tech investing. After a few years of developing investing fundamentals, she grew curious about startup operations. She spent time at a VC helping their portfolio companies scale, working with entrepreneurs on everything from fundraising to international expansion to sales. Along the way, Shilpa stumbled across venture studios and was immediately drawn to the model. She loves the magic of systematically building startups by combining an investor's mindset, passion for entrepreneurship, and operational acumen. Shilpa is now developing her product chops at Amazon. In the future, she hopes to use these critical skills to start her own venture studio.

A recent transplant to Seattle from the Bay Area, Shilpa is slowly growing accustomed to the cloudy Pacific Northwest. She loves playing tennis, drinking good coffee, and crocheting on rainy days.

Shilpa graduated Summa Cum Laude from the University of Pennsylvania. She holds a Bachelor of Science in Economics from The Wharton School and a Bachelor of Applied Science in Computer Science from the School of Engineering and Applied Science.

References

Riley, P. (2020). *The Rise of Startup Studios* [White paper]. Global Startup Studio Network (GSSN). https://www.gan.co/rise-startup-studios-white-paper/

Zasowski, N. (2020). *Disrupting the Venture Landscape* [White paper]. Global Startup Studio Network (GSSN). https://www.gan.co/wp-content/uploads/GSSN_StudioCapitalEfficiency_whitepaper.pdf

Nickmans, Q. (2020, June 2). Launching a Startup Studio: How to Finance It? *Inside eFounders*. https://blog.efounders.co/launching-a-startup-studio-how-to-finance-it-d847bbc11477

Carbrey, J. (2020, March 10). Understanding Startup Studio Structures. *FutureSight*. https://medium.com/futuresight/understanding-startup-studio-structures-e4482dd3b6a9

Szigeti, A. (2016). *Anatomy of Startup Studios: A behind the scenes look at how successful venture builders operate*. https://www.amazon.com/Anatomy-Startup-Studios-successful-builders-ebook/dp/B01BQOE89M

Szigeti, A (2019). *Startup Studio Playbook: For entrepreneurs, pioneers and creators who want to build ventures faster and with higher chance of success. Master the studio framework and start building*. https://www.amazon.com/Startup-Studio-Playbook-entrepreneurs-framework-ebook/dp/B07NVNYM4C

NVCA. (2021, March 15). *Record Year for U.S. Venture Capital Industry Despite Pandemic and Economic Downturn* [Press release]. https://nvca.org/pressreleases/record-year-for-u-s-venture-capital-industry-despite-pandemic-and-economic-downturn/

Lesage, D. (2020, July 8). The Real Difference Between Incubators and Startup Studios. *Dianna Lesage.* https://roamy.medium.com/the-real-difference-between-incubators-and-startup-studios-8175482697da

Prater, M. (2019, July 5). Incubator vs. Accelerator: What's the Difference? *HubSpot.* https://blog.hubspot.com/sales/incubator-vs-accelerator

NVCA. (2021). *NVCA Yearbook* [White paper]. https://nvca.org/wp-content/uploads/2021/08/NVCA-2021-Yearbook.pdf

Davis, A. (2021, October 17). These 6 charts show how much VC is awash in capital in 2021. *PitchBook.* https://pitchbook.com/news/articles/2021-us-vc-fundraising-exits-deal-flow-charts

Christensen, C. (2015, December). What is Disruptive Innovation? *Harvard Business Review.* https://hbr.org/2015/12/what-is-disruptive-innovation

Wagner, P. (2021, May 15). "The Sharpest of Recoveries": The 2021 V21 Analysis. *Wing.vc.* https://www.wing.vc/content/the-sharpest-of-recoveries-the-2021-v21-analysis

Y Combinator. (2021). *Series A Guide.* https://www.ycombinator.com/library/1l-round-size

Cambridge Associates. (2019, June 30). *US Venture Capital Index and Selected Benchmark Statistics.* [White paper]. https://www.cambridgeassociates.com/wp-content/uploads/2019/11/WEB-2019-Q2-USVC-Benchmark-Book.pdf

Glossary

Listed in order of relative appearance throughout the book.

Venture capital (VC)	Capital invested in an early high growth, often high risk, company in exchange for partial ownership
Seed	First round of startup funding
Series A, B, C, etc.	Subsequent rounds of startup funding (Series A being the earliest post-Seed, then B, etc.)
Pro-rata	Right for investors to participate in subsequent funding rounds to maintain their level of ownership percentage
KPI	Key performance indicator
LOI	Letter of intent
M&A	Merger and acquisition
IPO	Initial public offering
B2B	Business to business, as in a business model
SaaS	Software as a service, as in a vertical
D2C	Direct to consumer, as in a business model
MVP	Minimum viable product
LP	Limited partner
GP	General partner
IRR	Internal rate of return
MoM	Multiple of money (invested)

Made in the USA
Coppell, TX
07 June 2022

78555808R10090